FALLING IN LOVE WITH GOD'S WORD

Discovering What God
Always Intended Bible Study to Be

KEITH FERRIN

That You May Know Ministries

TYMK

This book is dedicated to Sarah Elizabeth.

You were born as these pages were being written.

May you grow to love God and

His wondrous Word.

I love you,
Dad

CONTENTS

THE NEXT STEP
Internalization

APPENDIXES

ACKNOWLEDGEMENTS

This book has been "in the works" for a long time. Several people have helped me tremendously at various stages.

Scott Gilchrist – You introduced me to much of the "method" contained in this book. Your passion for God's Word is unparalleled. Thank you for your inspiration, encouragement, and continued friendship.

Bruce Kuhn – I can't thank you enough for bringing the Word to life for me on that spring evening in 1993. Who knew God would use your presentation of Luke to propel me onto an entirely new ministry path?

Pete, Ron, Bruce, Pat, Scott, Murry, Kevin, and **Kari** – Thank you for the time you spent reading the original manuscript. Your suggestions helped make this material much more useful and accessible.

Brian Gage – Once again, you amaze me with your creativity and ability to take what little direction I give and come up with a design better than I could imagine.

Gary Thomas – Your input into the process of writing a book – from the encouragement to do it all the way to pointing me to a good printer – has been invaluable.

Nicole Zinn – For the countless hours you spent editing – and reediting – these pages, my gratitude is endless. Your fingerprint is on every page – from the overall structure to individual words. And thank you Caleb and Andrew, for waiting to be born until your mom was done with my book.

Kari – You've encouraged me to write, teach, speak, and perform for almost a decade. I can think of nothing I would rather do than make a home with you where God is glorified and His Word is loved. I love you.

Lord Jesus – You are the only true Author. Thank You for Your Word in all its forms – from the Word You used to speak creation into existence, to Your written Word, to You, the living, incarnate Word. Anything of worth contained between these two covers is from You, through You, and to You. I thank You and praise You.

IS IT POSSIBLE TO FALL IN LOVE WITH GOD'S WORD?

Introduction

Dear Reader,

Since you have this book in your hands, I imagine that you hope the answer to this question is "Yes!" Let me assure you that it is. Although I became a Christian as a young boy, I would not have described my relationship with the Bible using the word "love" until 1993. There are several specific things that happened between 1993 and 1997 that contributed greatly to my own experience of falling in love with God's Word.

The first of these events actually came in the form of a person. In 1993 I was working as the Pastor of Youth and Worship at a church in Western Washington. I was told of an actor named Bruce Kuhn who presented the entire Gospel of Luke – word-for-word – as a one-man play. Since Bruce was coming to a nearby church, I decided to check this out and see if someone could really memorize that much Scripture. I could not imagine straight Scripture engaging an audience for almost two hours.

I will never forget what happened that night. The Bible came to life. I heard Jesus talking with His disciples. I experienced the joy as a lame man jumped to his feet. I felt the pain as I witnessed Jesus' crucifixion. I *entered* the story.

When the presentation came to an end, I introduced myself to Bruce and asked if I could take him to lunch the next day. He accepted. As we talked, I inquired what it was like to have that much Scripture living inside him. He shared that the Bible and its characters were more real to him now than ever before. He also encouraged me to start memorizing larger portions of Scripture, rather than just a few verses here and there. I decided to start with something a bit shorter than the Gospel of Luke – Paul's letter to the Philippians.

I spent the summer and fall of 1993 soaking in Philippians. Over and over I read Paul's letter. One day I would pretend I was Paul writing the letter. The next day, I would picture myself sitting in the Church at Philippi on the day this letter was read. Before long, I found that I knew large portions of Philippians – and I hadn't even tried to memorize it yet! I also noticed that the Holy Spirit would frequently bring verses to my mind as I walked throughout my day. I came to realize that I hadn't simply memorized Philippians – I had *internalized* it. This letter was now a part of me. I not only knew the words, but I *understood* the message, *felt* the emotions, and *experienced* the relationships. "The Living Word of God" was no longer just a phrase. It was a *reality*! The benefits I discovered from internalizing Philippians spurred me on to a continuing journey of Scripture internalization that keeps getting more enjoyable and rewarding.

The second major event on my journey toward falling in love with God's Word came in 1997. This was the year I met Scott Gilchrist, a pastor from Beaverton, Oregon. Though I had already internalized Philippians and the Gospel of John at that point, I still did not have an organized method for studying a book of the Bible. Scott handed me a book titled *Mastering the Bible Book by Book* – written by a friend of his, Robert Shirock.[1] Scott used this book to introduced me to a method of Bible study that completely changed my understanding of – and love for – God's Word. I had never seen a method that walked through a process of getting to know a book of the Bible as a whole, all the way down to discovering the nuance of a particular word.

It was easy to see how this new study method perfectly complemented the Scripture Internalization I was already practicing. The combination has created a richer experience of God's Word than I had ever known. Much of that method is woven into the words on the following pages.

As I continued to develop this idea of weaving together Scripture Internalization with this new method of Bible Study, I had the opportunity to share it with many people individually. Some of these were pastors who asked if I would teach this process to the members of their congregations. I started to organize my thoughts, developed a workbook, and began teaching *Falling in Love with God's Word* as a workshop in 1998.

Since then, the challenge has been what to do when someone says to me, "My cousin Alice in South Dakota would love this." I didn't have a good way for someone to learn this approach outside the setting of a workshop. The workbook had been designed as a teaching aid for the workshop, not as a stand-alone training tool. You are holding my attempt at solving this dilemma.

While we will spend many of the pages that follow exploring word studies, outlining, and a host of other topics, getting you to understand and use a certain *method* is not my primary aim. My heart's desire is that you will find in this book some tools to help you fall in love with God's Word. If you come away viewing the Bible as simply a textbook full of information you need to know, then I have failed. The Bible is not a textbook – it is a *relationship guide*. God's desire is to continually develop your relationship with Him and He designed the Bible for just that purpose. My hope is that the tools in this book will enable you more and more to see the Bible as a living part of your relationship with its Author.

I expect that each reader will use this book a little differently. You might sift through these pages and find a couple nuggets that enhance a method of study you already find successful. Or you may have tried everything but never found a way to enjoy the Bible and be consistent with your time in God's Word. Appendix A outlines a 60-day Adventure in Philippians that provides a day-to-day guide for practicing each of the elements of this method, enabling you to experiment and incorporate the elements that work for you. I have also included different options or New Believers and Small Groups. (See Appendixes B & C)

Whether you plan on trying an option from one of the Appendixes or incorporating pieces of this method into what you already do, I encourage you to apply the techniques in this book *as you read*, rather than reading the book straight through and intending to apply them later. Anything new is best understood by utilizing small pieces as you learn.

Allow me to give you a few words of warning before we get started. First of all, if you have struggled with consistency in reading the Bible, please don't begin this book thinking it will instantly solve this problem. Spending time in the Bible is one of the most important and rewarding of life's pursuits. However, it is also a habit that must be developed over time, just as you would develop a habit of regular exercise or healthy eating. It is not easy, and it requires discipline. The last thing the devil wants is for you to be in God's Word everyday – let alone love it! - and he will do everything he can to convince you that it just isn't worth the time or effort. I can assure you that the rewards *far* outweigh the effort.

As a second word of warning, you will find as you read that there may be times when you begin to feel overwhelmed and think, "There is no way I can do this. It would take hours and hours everyday." It is important to remember that you won't be doing each element of this method everyday. Even if you decide to jump in with both feet and tackle the 60-Day Adventure in Philippians, I have broken down each day to be a 20- to 30-minute commitment.

As I write, these are my prayers: May you find yourself enjoying God's Word like never before. May His truths be evident to you. May the stories and people in the Bible leap off the pages. May you find yourself drawn to the heart of the One who wrote the Bible especially for you. May God use this book to help you fall in love with His Book.

Blessings,
Keith

WHAT DOES THE BIBLE SAY ABOUT HOW TO STUDY THE BIBLE?

Setting the Stage

†

A re you someone who likes to know why you are going to do something before you do it? I know I am. I don't mind working hard if I can see a reason for the task and know there will be a positive result when I'm finished. Running sprints is bearable when we realize that being in shape is going to prepare us for the game. Traveling for several hours is okay if we know that a vacation spot is waiting when we finally park the car. If the task we are working on will positively affect our company, we don't mind working diligently.

The same is true for Bible study. The purpose of this chapter is to give a *reason* for the method described in the bulk of these pages. When I see the people in the Bible *loving* it, *sharing* it, and *applying* it, I cannot help but want my attitude toward Scripture to mirror theirs. When we see how study and internalization leads to a deeper passion for God and His Word, we can look at Bible study as an exciting adventure, rather than merely an academic exercise.

We could spend this entire book looking at the Bible's references to itself. However, let's simply look at five lessons we can learn from a few passages in both the Old Testament and the New Testament.

Lesson 1: To truly love God with our whole being, we must integrate His Word into every area of our lives.

"Hear, O Israel: The Lord our God is one Lord. Love the Lord your God with all your heart and with all your soul and with all your strength."

- Deuteronomy 6:4-5

These are two of the most famous verses in all of Scripture. When Jesus was asked which was the greatest of all commandments, He quoted these words, spoken centuries earlier by Moses to the Israelites before entering the Promised Land. However, the problem these verses present to many of us is that they tell us *what* we are to do, but not *how* we can actually do it. I have good news though. As we keep reading, the verses that round out this paragraph provide five clear guidelines—within **Lesson 1**—that show us how to live out the command given in the first two verses.

1. *"These commandments that I give you today are to be upon your hearts."* (Verse 6)

To fully grasp the weight of this statement, it is crucial to understand the meaning of the Hebrew word for "heart" (lebab). To the Jewish people, the heart represented the totality of a person. They understood the heart to be the combined essence of the intellect, the emotions, and the will. In short, Moses was saying, "God's Word must saturate your entire being. Your thoughts should line up with the Word. Your emotions, wants, and desires need to be guided by the Word. Your choices must be made in accordance with the Word." Moses knew that devotion to God is not true devotion unless it is accompanied by a *life aligned with the Word of God.*

2. *"Impress them on your children."* (Verse 7a)

My family had several traditions. Starting a road trip with breakfast at McDonald's. Opening only one present on Christmas Eve. Many traditions occur once a year. Knowing and loving the Word of God, though, is a tradition to be passed down continually.

The Apostle Paul wrote of passing faith from generation to generation in his second letter to Timothy. *"I have been reminded of your sincere faith, which first lived in your grandmother Lois and in your mother Eunice and, I am persuaded, now lives in you also."* (II Timothy 1:5) Timothy's heritage of faithfulness went back at least two generations.

Passing down a love for God's Word does not mean force-feeding Bible verses to our kids. Rather, the best way to "impress" a love for the Word on our children is to have them see us loving the Word and living accordingly. If the Bible is exciting, valuable, and applicable to us, the likelihood is that it will be so for them as well. We need to have our children see us not only studying God's Word, but *enjoying* it and *integrating* it into our daily lives.

My family had its problems and quirks – like yours, I would guess – but there is one thing I am very thankful for: My parents raised me to believe that following Jesus, going to church, and reading the Bible were not only necessary – but enjoyable! If you were raised believing the same things, take time to give thanks. If not, make a commitment now to pass on a love for God and His Word to the next generation.

3. *"Talk about them when you sit at home and when you walk along the road, when you lie down and when you get up."* (Verse 7b)

How often do you discuss the Bible with friends and family? If the only time we talk about the Bible is when we're at church, how do we expect the promises and commands in it to permeate our everyday lives? We need to study the Bible in a way that allows the Holy Spirit to use the Word to shape our speech.

The more I discuss any given topic, the more interested I become. I understand the topic more and gain new insights from discussions with others. The same holds true for the Bible. Other viewpoints illuminate truths I would never have seen on my own. As we talk about God's Word we discover what passages someone else finds enriching, confusing, challenging, or encouraging. A passage that is confusing to me might be one that you understand – and vice versa. How can we help each other understand a passage if we don't know the portions each of us struggles with? We need to heed the advice found in Proverbs 27:17: *"As iron sharpens iron, A friend sharpens a friend."* (NLT)

While talking about the Bible is vitally important, this command is much broader than simply having discussions about the Bible. God also wants us to make sure our speech lines up with His Word. This might be one of the greatest challenges of living life as a Christian. Do you struggle with this? I know I sure do. Do you find it difficult to refrain from sharing the latest gossip? Do you find yourself speaking differently around people at work than people at church? Do you use language at school or with friends that you would never use around your mother? Sadly, I must admit I have struggled (or continue to struggle) with all of these at one time or another.

James, Jesus' brother, knew this was a difficult issue as well. He described the tongue as *"…a fire, A world of evil among the parts of the body. It corrupts the whole person, sets the whole course of his life on fire, and is itself set on fire by hell."* (James 3:6) Yikes! Not an easy description to brush aside. However, James also has high praise for the words we speak when he says, *"If anyone is never at fault in what he says, he is a perfect man, able to keep his whole body in check."* (James 3:2) He goes on to compare the tongue to a rudder that is small, but able to guide a large ship.

Jesus brings this whole topic back to a "heart issue" when He says, *"the good man brings good things out of the good stored up in his heart, and the evil man brings evil things out of the evil stored up in his heart. **For out of the overflow of his heart his mouth speaks.**"* (Luke 6:45, *emphasis mine*) The first command in this section told us that God's Word is to "be upon our hearts." The more we take in His Word – and talk about it – the more likely it will be for His words to come out when we open our mouths.

4. *"Tie them as symbols on your hands and bind them on your foreheads."* (Verse 8)

Unless you know a little about ancient Jewish culture, this guideline and the next might seem a bit strange. At the time Moses was saying these words (15th Century B.C.), not everyone had their own copy of a Bible. There were, however, portions of

Scripture that were believed to be so important that each person should have access to these verses at all times. The verses were written down, wrapped up and either tied to the left arm or put in little boxes (called phylacteries) and worn on the forehead. As a result, any passerby could recognize a Jew just by looking for a phylactery.

This brings us to the message of this verse: If someone looked at your life, would they immediately see someone striving to live life in line with the Word of God? No matter whom your friends are, what your family is like, where you live, or what kind of job you have, one common characteristic of those who truly love God is a desire to live our lives – individually – in accordance with the Word.

5. "Write them on the doorframes of your houses and on your gates." (Verse 9)

This guideline is similar to the last – with a little twist. Just as hands and foreheads belong to an individual, doorframes and gates typically identify places where there are *groups* of people. This verse emphasizes the importance of surrounding ourselves with people who desire to walk in obedience to God's Word.

Before going on, I want to make it clear that this command does not mean we must abandon our non-believing friends. Jesus himself said that we are to "Go and make disciples..." (Mt. 28:19), and we can hardly accomplish that only among our friends who already believe. Having said that, we must make sure that our *intimate* friendships are with people who love the Lord. We are asking for trouble if the people we go to for advice about life decisions have no intention of seeking God's guidance before offering their counsel. We must place ourselves in the midst of people who will encourage us in our desire to follow Christ.

In Deuteronomy 6:4-9, God provides us with five guidelines for loving Him with everything we've got.

1. *Let God's Word be upon your heart.*
2. *Pass on a love for the Word to the next generation.*
3. *Allow the Word to shape your speech.*
4. *Strive to live your life – as an individual –
   in accordance with the Word.*
5. *Surround yourself with people who are also seeking
   to live according to the Word.*

Verses 4-5 command us to love God with all our heart, soul, and strength. Verses 6-9 show us that to carry out this command the Word must saturate every part of our lives – inside and out. This compels us to find a way to study the Bible that will enable us not only to know and remember what it says, but also to love it enough to incorporate it into our lives.

Lesson 2: To integrate God's Word into our lives, we must know it well enough that we can think about it even when our Bibles are not open in front of us.

"Do not let this book of the law depart from your mouth; meditate on it day and night, so that you may be

careful to do everything written in it. Then you will be prosperous and successful. Have I not commanded you? Be strong and courageous. Do not be terrified; do not be discouraged, for the Lord your God will be with you wherever you go."

- Joshua 1:8-9

What do you think of when you hear the word "meditate?" In our culture, most of us probably picture someone sitting on the floor with crossed legs and closed eyes, making strange noises. That isn't exactly the picture God is painting when He uses this word as He speaks to Joshua before leading him into battle with the Canaanites. To be fair, part of the meaning of the Hebrew word used here is "to moan, utter, or speak." This was a low volume form of speaking the words of Scripture as a way to focus on God in the midst of many battling thoughts. The Greek equivalent to this word means to "revolve around in the mind." The idea behind all this is to plant God's Word so deeply into our hearts and minds that we can ponder His words as we walk throughout the busyness of our days.

Joshua had a huge task before him. After wandering in the desert for forty years, he was about to lead the Israelites into the Promised Land. The people living there, however, were hardly about to hand over their land to a group of Israelite nomads. This land would have to be taken by force.

It is in the midst of this impending battle that God tells Joshua to keep His Word on the tip of his tongue and at the forefront of his thinking. The reason? Joshua was about to encounter distractions from every side. God wanted Joshua to remember that even in the midst of battle, he was called to *"be careful to do everything written"* in God's Word. He could only live up to that calling if God's Word permeated his thoughts and words.

The same is true for us. While our battle is different from Joshua's, our distractions are just as real. How can we live a life of obedience to God if we only know what His commands are during the few minutes we have our Bibles open in front of us?

These two verses also offer three wonderfully encouraging promises about what will happen when we are careful to live our lives according to God's Word. First, we will be prosperous and successful. Be careful not to use these verses to develop a theory that says, "Obey God and life will be smooth sailing, filled with material blessings." God's idea of "prosperous and successful" is rarely the same as society's. God is more concerned about our *internal* and *eternal* success, than our external success. Second, meditating on and following God's Word will increase our courage and decrease our fear. We can boldly live life – free from fear – if we know that we are living in accordance with God's will. Lastly, and most encouraging, meditating on the Word is a constant reminder that the Lord is with us wherever we go. Encouragement indeed!

Lesson 3: Bible Study + Scripture Internalization = A Love for God's Word.

> *"How can a young man keep his way pure?*
> *By living according to your word.*
> *I seek you with all my heart;*

do not let me stray from your commands.
I have hidden your word in my heart
   that I might not sin against you.
Praise be to you, O Lord;
   teach me your decrees.
With my lips I recount
   all the laws that come from your mouth.
I rejoice in following your statutes
   as one rejoices in great riches.
I meditate on your precepts
   and consider your ways.
I delight in your decrees;
   I will not neglect your word."

"Oh, how I love your law!
   I meditate on it all day long."
                                    - Psalm 119:9-16, 97

Take a look at that last statement again. Every time I read this verse I am struck not only by David's enthusiastic love, but also by the *object* of his love. If I had written this sentence, I am certain I would have replaced the word "law" with "faithfulness," "mercy," "kindness," or "goodness." But David exclaims with joyful exuberance, *"Oh, how I love your law!"* David is infatuated with God's Word. David then tells God that he keeps His words revolving around in his mind all day long. We need to be doing precisely the same thing – with precisely the same attitude.

Earlier in this passage, David talks about technique and attitude when handling God's Word. Three of the statements he makes have to do with a deep study of the Word. *"I seek You…"* *"Teach me Your decrees."* *"I will not neglect Your Word."* David knew that he needed to be diligent in seeking after the things of God found in Scripture. However, he also recognized the need to internalize the Word – not just study it. Notice these three phrases: *"I have hidden Your Word in my heart,"* *"With my lips I recount…,"* and *"I meditate…and consider…"* These elements of internalization are essential to our time in God's Word if we are to develop a deep sense of love for the Bible.

Finally, David uses the words "rejoice" and "delight" to describe his experience of and interaction with the truths he finds in Scripture. In fact, he talks of rejoicing in obeying God's Word "as one rejoices in great riches." We hear words like "law", "statutes," and "decrees," and we may be tempted to picture the Bible as a list of "Dos" and "Don'ts." Although the Bible is so much more than such a list, I no longer apologize for the "Dos" and "Don'ts" that it *does* contain. We can rejoice – along with David – that the Author of Life has given us a Guidebook, pointing out what to avoid and what to jump into with both feet. After all, Jesus himself said, *"I have come that they may have life, and that they may have it more abundantly."* (John 10:10 NKJV)

When we study, speak, and soak in the Scriptures we will find ourselves loving – and obeying – God's Word with the same enthusiastic passion as David. We will also be well on our way to experiencing the abundant life Jesus longs for us to have.

Lesson 4: The Bible is useful and essential for developing a healthy, strong faith.

> *"All Scripture is God-breathed and is useful for teaching, rebuking, correcting, and training in righteousness, so that the man of God may be thoroughly equipped for every good work."*
>
> - II Timothy 3:16-17

I remember the first time I went to lift weights in the high school weight room. I was ready to get muscles that would rip my shirt just by flexing. (Okay, so I watched one too many episodes of "The Incredible Hulk" as a kid.) Over to the bench press I went. I put a few weights on the bar, flopped down on the bench, and lifted the bar into the air. One. No problem. Two. They say this is hard? Three. Still going strong. I think by about the seventh or eighth rep, one of the guys from the other side of the room (you know, the ones who actually *have* muscles) must have noticed my face changing various shades of purple. He said, "Hey! Breathe!" Useful tip. I was focused so intently on lifting the weight, I had forgotten to breathe while I lifted.

As Paul wrote his last letter to Timothy, he wanted to remind Timothy that Scripture is the very breath of God. We have the opportunity to inhale God's breath every day. If you want to build up your "spiritual muscles," inhaling deeply of God's Word is essential. Our physical muscles need oxygen to grow and serve us effectively. Our faith needs the oxygen of Scripture to grow and enable us to serve God effectively.

Many in our society would have us believe the Bible is a book filled with outdated stories and outdated values that applied to people who lived in an outdated time. Nothing could be further from the truth. As long as the Bible is useful for teaching, rebuking, correcting, and training in righteousness, we need to read it, study it, and internalize it. Not too long ago, I heard someone share an analogy that shed new light on this verse for me. He compared the life God calls us to live to a path. He went on to say that *teaching* tells us what that path is. *Rebuking* shows us where we've gotten off the path. *Correcting* informs us how to get back on the path. And *training in righteousness* is how we stay on the path once we get back on.

All of us are in one of these four places in relation to the path at any given time. This verse lets us know that God's Word is useful wherever you happen to find yourself. One final reminder as you walk along the path: Don't forget to breathe!

Lesson 5: Internalizing the Word helps us both to share the Word with others and to receive the Word with enthusiasm and understanding.

"As his custom was, Paul went into the synagogue, and on three Sabbath days he reasoned with them from the Scriptures, explaining and proving that the Christ had to suffer and rise from the dead. 'This Jesus I am proclaiming to you is the Christ,' he said."

"Now the Bereans were of more noble character than the Thessalonians, for they received the message with great

eagerness and examined the Scriptures every day to see if what Paul said was true."

- Acts 17:2-3 & 11

Have you ever had one of those "light bulb" experiences? You know the ones. Someone is explaining something and you just don't get it. They try one angle. You still don't get it. They come at it from another side. Still isn't clicking. Then they say or do something and the light bulb comes on. You get it!

I believe that most non-believers are one light bulb experience away from following Christ. I think Paul felt the same way. That's why, week after week, he would come back to the same place and "reason with them from the Scriptures." He knew that he held the Truth that could set them free. He did not want to give up until their light bulbs came on. For some, all he had to do was *explain* the good news about Jesus to them. Others needed *proof* that Jesus was the long-awaited Messiah.

Either way, Paul's method was the same – let the Scriptures speak for themselves. We would do well to follow his example. Peter says in I Peter 3:15, *"Always be prepared to give an answer to everyone who asks you to give the reason for the hope that you have. But do this with gentleness and respect."* We need to study the Bible in such a way that the Holy Spirit can access His Word inside us when the opportunity arises for us to explain or prove to someone what we know to be true about Jesus.

There is also a lesson to be learned in this passage from the Bereans. These people of noble character knew the importance of internalizing Scripture. When they heard Paul saying things that resonated with what they already knew, they "received the message with great eagerness." Has that ever happened to you? You go to church, only to have the pastor preach on the very things you were reading earlier that week. How exciting! God is not in the habit of revealing His truth only to a select few who preach sermons or write books. He desires to reveal Himself to all who would fall in love with His Word.

The Bereans however, did not accept Paul's message blindly. They understood that Paul was simply a man. He was not divine. Although Paul sought earnestly to portray Christ accurately, he was not a perfectly accurate representation of God. Only Christ is. Therefore, the Bereans accepted the message eagerly, but *also* dove deeply into the Scriptures themselves. No teacher, no matter how godly and sincere, is outside of the reach of sin and error. If we do not study the Word for ourselves, we have cheated the true Teacher out of an opportunity to reveal Himself to us.

Internalizing Scripture equips us for both occasions: when God beckons us to be the sharers of truth, as well as when He would have someone else share truth with us.

Five Lessons the Bible teaches about itself:

1. *To truly love God with our whole being, we must integrate the Word into every area of our lives.*
2. *To truly meditate on God's Word, we must know it well enough that we can think about it at times other than when we have our Bible open in front of us.*
3. *Bible Study + Scripture Internalization = A Love for God's Word.*
4. *The Bible is useful and essential for developing a healthy, strong faith.*
5. *Internalizing the Word helps us both to share the Word with others and receive the Word with enthusiasm and understanding.*

As we read the passages mentioned in this chapter, I am struck by the prevailing thought woven throughout each:

To love and obey God with our whole being, we must internalize His Word in such a way that allows God to use His Word to shape all that we are, say, do, and think.

To finish setting the stage for the method in the remaining pages, I think it is worthwhile to take a look at two passages of Scripture side-by-side.[1] Both of these passages were written by the Apostle Paul. Read each of them and note the similarities.

Ephesians 5:18-20 *"Spirit-filled"*	Colossians 3:16-17 *"Word-Filled"*
Instead, be filled with the Spirit.	Let the Word of Christ dwell in you richly...
Speak to one another...	...as you teach and admonish one another with all wisdom,
...with psalms, hymns and spiritual songs. Sing and make music...	...and as you sing psalms, hymns and spiritual songs...
...with your heart to the Lord,	...with gratitude in your hearts to God.
...always giving thanks to God the Father for everything, in the name of our Lord Jesus Christ.	And whatever you do, whether in word or deed, do it all in the name of the Lord Jesus, giving thanks to God the Father through Him.

As Paul talks about a "Spirit-filled" life in Ephesians and a "Word-filled" life in Colossians, he uses almost the exact same wording. In our churches, we frequently hear the phrase "Spirit-filled," but I don't think I have ever heard anyone say, "Hey. You see that gal over there. She sure is a Word-filled Christian." Why not? Paul knew these two characteristics are so closely related that he could barely find different words to describe them!

The Holy Spirit certainly speaks to us in more ways than just through the words of the Bible. He speaks to us as we pray, as He brings certain thoughts to mind, as He inspires others to share with us at our point of need, and in a whole host of other ways. However, all of His leading will be *consistent* with what is written in the Bible. For us to distinguish His voice from all the other voices that crowd our minds, we must regularly internalize God's Word. A pastor I know once said, "There are times when thoughts and dreams are directly given by the Holy Spirit. There are other times when they're just the result of bad pizza. Make sure you know the difference." The more richly the Word is dwelling in us, the easier it is to make that distinction.

WHERE ARE WE HEADING?

Overview of the Process

M y wife and I recently built a house. As I look back on the whole process, I am struck by the similarities between how our house was built and the method I am about to show you for studying the Bible.

The first step in the process was actually taken long before any construction began. We started by answering some very important questions: Is this where we want to live? What is the cost going to be? Can we afford it? What do we think about the land? Is the house going to meet our needs now and into the future? How do the time, effort and cost of building a home compare to simply buying one – and will building be worth it?

It was crucial to answer all of these questions. Answering these "What" and "Why" questions is what the *Setting the Stage* section was all about. What does the Bible say about itself – and how to study it? Why should we put the effort into internalizing God's Word? Is it worth it?

Now it's time to move on to the "How" question. Looking back to the construction of our home, I now see that everything happened in three consecutive phases: Foundation, Framing, and Finish Work. "Building" our knowledge of a book of the Bible follows the same pattern.

Foundation

No one who has built a house doubts the necessity of a solid foundation. The rest of the home is built on top of the foundation and falls within its constraints. Many of the home's identifying features will be determined by the size, shape and strength of the foundation. The foundation's strength will also be a key factor in the home's lifespan.

During the *Foundation Phase* of Bible Study we get to know a book of the Bible as a whole unit. What is the storyline? Who wrote the book? To whom was he writing? What is the primary purpose? We build our "foundation" of knowledge by reading the book in general terms and exploring the background. Only when a good foundation has been laid are we ready to start "framing."

Framing

I was amazed at how fast the framing went on our house. In the span of a week, we went from looking at a cement foundation to walking through the "rooms" of our house. The framing process joined everything together: electrical, plumbing, windows, doors, and sheetrock. Equally important is that the framing is what attached all of it to the foundation and made it secure.

While it didn't take long, framing represented an essential transition. The same is true for the *Framing Phase* of Bible study. The general approach of *Foundation* and the detailed approach of *Finish Work* are held together by the *Framing Phase*. Framing establishes an outline of a book, breaking it down into sections that can be explored one day at a time.

Finish Work

As our house neared completion, we were excited to see each new little piece as it was completed. How rewarding to see it all come together! By the time we moved in, I felt like I knew that house inside and out. I had seen the wiring go in. I was there when the paint was applied. I saw many of the light fixtures hung. Exploring the details – one right after another – added an appreciation for our house that stays with me still.

The Finish Work Phase is just as important to the Bible study process. Studying paragraphs, words and phrases, and making life application will cause you to fall in love with God's Word on a very deep and intimate level.

Internalization

When you've internalized a portion of Scripture you feel like you "own" it, rather than simply "know" it. To follow our construction analogy, someone else could build a home exactly like ours, and yet it would *feel* different because Kari and I have personalized it. Throughout the construction we made specific choices about fixtures, lighting, etc. that another couple might not have chosen. Also, the personalizing of our home continues today, and will continue as our family grows.

Likewise, the process of internalization is both woven throughout the three phases of *Foundation, Framing,* and *Finish Work,* and continues for months and years after a specific, dedicated period of studying a book of the Bible. It is *not* simply a list of "memorization techniques." Although there are some specific tools for helping you get the words right, it is really about keeping our focus on knowing the *Word*, not simply knowing the *words*.

> *Note: As we walk through each section, it may be helpful to occasionally flip back to Appendix A and see how each element is placed into the 60-day Adventure in Philippians.*

PHASE ONE

Foundation

THE BEAUTY OF THE BIG PICTURE

Foundation

Picture this scene. You're sitting in a job interview. The interviewer begins by asking if you have any questions before he starts in with his own. Your first questions are: Where is the copy room? What does the guy over there do? How does that machine work? What time is lunch?

After answering several questions, the interviewer gives you a strange look and says, "Do you even know what we *do* here?" You reply, "No. I just like to get all the details right away. I'll make sense of them later."

Of course this scenario is absurd. When you apply for a job, your first inclination is to find out about the product or service the company offers. Only then do you start to look at details. This is the same for almost every area of our lives. Even if you think of yourself as a "details" person, you probably still like to have a general understanding of something before being bombarded with specifics. We long for the Big Picture. Why? *Because details only make sense in light of the Big Picture.*

I have spent about thirteen years of my life involved in soccer, either on the field as a player or on the sidelines as a coach. If you have been around a soccer field very often, then you understand the terms "trapping," "half-volley," "diamond defense," or "drawing the Striker off sides". If you are completely confused right now, then I should probably start by telling you that soccer is a game where twenty-two players run around a lot, trying to kick a ball into the other team's goal. And by the way, they do all this without using their hands. After you understand soccer in *general terms*, then we can move on to *specific* terminology and strategy.

You might be wondering what soccer has to do with Bible study. The Foundation Phase, is the part of the Bible study process that paints the Big Picture in our minds before we dive into the details. During the Foundation Phase, we take a book – or large passage – of the Bible and look at all the individual parts as a single, coherent whole. This type of general study has seven primary benefits:

1. *The Foundation Phase helps you develop a love for the book as a whole.*

2. *The Foundation Phase gives you an historical overview of the book and helps you to understand the author's thought process.*

3. *The Foundation Phase helps you identify the book's purpose. Understanding a book's purpose enables you to more effectively remember – and share – any part of that book, and also provides additional insight as you move into in-depth study.*

4. *The Foundation Phase gives you a feel for the relationship between the book's author and its intended audience or recipients. (Many books of the Bible are actually letters.)*

5. *The Foundation Phase helps you to understand the setting in which a book of the Bible was written. Grasping the*

setting gives you a greater appreciation for and understand ing of the book's message.

6. *The Foundation Phase prepares your mind and heart to internalize Scripture.*

7. *The Foundation Phase lays a solid base that tremendously enhances any further, in-depth study (Framing and Finish Work).*

The Foundation Phase – combined with the short Framing Phase – makes up the first 30 days of the complete Bible study process. (See Appendix A: A 60-Day Adventure in Philippians.) In the rest of this section we'll explore the three elements of the Foundation Phase[1]:

- Foundational Reading
- Background Studies
- Purpose Statement

IS THERE
A RIGHT WAY
TO READ THE BIBLE?

Foundational Reading

Have you ever found your mind wandering as you read your Bible? Do you ever finish reading and find yourself unable to remember what you read? I don't know about you, but I find this very frustrating. After all, this is *God's Word!* Shouldn't it be the most exciting thing we read?

The issue that keeps most of us from really engaging with and learning to love the Bible is that most of us don't read it *correctly*. Here's what I mean. Think of your favorite author – maybe a mystery or biography writer, or an expert on your favorite subject. Once you have read and enjoyed several books by that author, you start to eagerly anticipate the next book. You expect it to be great.

Did you catch that? You *expect* the next book to be great. Many of us *want* the Bible to be exciting, but we don't really *expect* it to be. We all know the power of expectation. If you go to a party expecting to have a good time, you will be more likely to actually have a good time than if you go thinking the party will be dull. If you go into a test expecting to miss every question, the probability of passing the test with flying colors is quite slim. The next time you sit down to read your Bible, try to read with an expectation that the God of the Universe wants your time in His Word to be exciting – because He does!

Never forget that your time reading your Bible is time with Him. The primary objective of this book is *not* to give you a method to follow or an academic exercise to employ. Bible study is primarily *relationship* time. The technique must always be secondary to the relationship. You and I have the chance to get to know the Author. He wants to spend time with us. Reading the Word must always be about relationship with God, not just information about God.

The five elements of Foundational Reading[1] are:

1. *Prayerful Reading*
2. *Continuous Reading*
3. *Repetitious Reading*
4. *Independent Reading*
5. *Thoughtful Reading*

Rather than being progressive steps, these elements are principles we can practice simultaneously to transform our time in the Word.

Prayerful Reading

Imagine for a minute that you are a running back for a football team. (For some of us that's a big stretch, but bear with me.) Your team is starting on the 20-yard line. Eighty yards to go. Your goal is to get to the end zone. You've prepared. You know the play. You are completely committed to getting to the end zone. The ball is snapped and placed right in your hands. Off you go. Five yards down the field – boom! – you're knocked right on your backside. As you lay there on the ground you think to yourself, "Hmmm. Why am I not in the end zone? Why did I only get five yards down the field? I was totally ready. I don't understand." Finally, a little voice in your head says, "Because there's someone playing defense!"

Do you realize that there is someone playing "defense" while you are trying to read the Bible? There is someone who wants you *not* to have quality time with God as much as (or more than) you want to have it. In his first letter, Peter warns, *"Be self-controlled and alert. Your enemy the devil prowls around like a roaring lion looking for someone to devour."* (I Peter 5:8) The Enemy is doing everything he can to distract you – or better yet – convince you that you are too busy to spend time with God at all! We need to be ready for the distractions. We need to prepare in advance to deal with any excuse for not spending time in the Word. We all need an "offensive" attack to deal with the devil's defense.

That is why Prayerful Reading is vitally important. We simply don't have the strength to fight a spiritual battle without the help of the Holy Spirit. In Ephesians 6, right after Paul has finished listing all the pieces of the "full armor of God," he makes this statement: *"And pray in the Spirit on all occasions with all kinds of prayers and requests. With this in mind, be alert and always keep on praying for all the saints."* (Eph. 6:18)

Whenever you set out to spend time in the Word, take some time to ask God to help keep your mind focused, to reveal His Word to you, and to help you fall more deeply in love with Him and His Word. Then, as you read, if you find your mind wandering, stop and spend some time in prayer again. It may be that a short, one-sentence prayer is all you need to refocus, or it could be that God is urging you to simply stop reading and focus on Him for a while. Either way, the goal is to build your relationship with God, not simply to get through your reading for the day. As you come to the end of your time in the Word, pray again, asking the Holy Spirit to keep your mind focused on Him – and the passages you have read – as you go throughout your day.

The Enemy wants to keep you from spending time with God in His Word. And if you do set aside time for Bible study, he most certainly does not want it to be fruitful. However, your Heavenly Father wants nothing more than to build a vibrant, meaningful relationship with you. He wants you to love spending time in His Word and He is able to make that a reality in your life.

As I mentioned earlier, Bible study is primarily relationship time. Approaching God's Word with a prayerful attitude is the first step toward entering His presence. Our desire must be to not only learn about God, but also to hear from Him, talk to Him, know Him more intimately. Simply put – we need to be with Him. Prayerful Reading is the key ingredient in fostering that relationship. It is also essential if you want to develop a love for His Word.

Continuous Reading

When was the last time you sat down and read an entire book of the Bible in one sitting? For the first twenty years I was a Christian, I never had. I never even considered it. I had been told somewhere along the line that I should read a chapter a day. Where did that idea ever come from? Not that reading a chapter a day is bad, but it certainly won't make the Bible come alive. Could you imagine picking up a novel by your favorite author and only reading one or two pages a day? It wouldn't matter how talented the author was; that would be one boring novel!

Reading a chapter of the Bible typically takes between two and five minutes. If that is all the time we spend reading the Bible, it is no wonder that three hours later we can't remember what we read. We need to read the Bible in such a way that the entire message sticks in our head once the Bible is closed and we are going about our daily business.

Continuous Reading means reading a complete book of the Bible in one sitting. You may be thinking, "That would take hours!" Actually, there are more books of the Bible that can be read – in their entirety – in less than thirty minutes than there are books that take more than thirty minutes. Obviously, there are some books that would take much more time, such as the Gospels, Genesis, and several others. With these books, I suggest breaking them down into larger chunks, so that you end up reading the whole book over the course of a week or a few days.

The purpose of Continuous Reading is to get a feel for the book as a whole. It provides you with a good understanding of the general message. You are not examining every detail – yet. The Finish Work Phase is the time for that. Remember: for now, you are looking at the Big Picture.

Repetitious Reading

Once you have read through a book of the Bible, try this the next day: read it again! And again the next day. And again the next day. If our goal is to hide God's Word in our hearts, we are going to have to soak in it. This principal is not unique to Bible study. It is simply the way our brains work; we need repetition. This is why pianists practice the same song over and over until it is second nature. And why golfers hit buckets and buckets of balls on the driving range. Repetition makes things stick.

Whenever you set out to study a new book of the Bible, a good goal is to start by reading that book thirty times in thirty days. That may sound like a lot, but one month from now you could know a book of the Bible better than you have ever known one before. That is the power of Repetitious Reading! It plants the stories and concepts firmly in your mind, so that when you begin to study verse by verse, you already have the context of those verses planted in your memory.

Obviously, with the longer books of the Bible, you will not be able to read them thirty times in thirty days. However, most of these are books that tell a story and do not take quite the amount of repetition to gain a good understanding of the plotline, characters, and events. For these books, I would still recommend reading them through a few times over the course of a month before you dive into any verse-by-verse study.

Though you may initially think that Repetitious Reading must get boring, you will actually find that when you start to understand the verses and the way they fit together, the Bible will hold more meaning and excitement for you than ever before. I have found that the last fifteen days of reading are actually more exciting than the first fifteen days.

In order to more firmly cement the Scripture into your mind, make sure that during Repetitious Reading you read the same Bible every day. Not just the same Bible translation, but the same physical Bible. That may sound strange, but using the same Bible will actually help you to internalize Scripture without even trying. You will start to notice that you automatically remember where certain verses are located on a page.

At a few specific times during the Foundation Phase – about every five to seven days – purposefully read a different translation of the Bible. This will give you a fresh look at the book. Sometimes a different wording will shed some light on a passage that did not make sense to you before. After reading the new translation, return to your primary Study Bible the next day. You will add this new insight into the passages that are now becoming familiar to you.

Before we move on, allow me to encourage you not to underestimate the importance of Repetitious Reading. After ten or eleven days, you may be tempted to say, "Okay, I know this. I can move on." If you really want God's Word to stay with you for the long haul, make sure you stick with it for the whole thirty days.

Independent Reading

When you read your Bible, are you constantly glancing at the notes at the bottom of the page or looking in a commentary to find out what a passage means? Let me start out by saying that commentaries, Study Bible notes, and other reference materials are invaluable tools. However, many of us rely on this information before we even *try* to understand a passage by ourselves. It is as if we subtly tell ourselves, "I can't understand the Bible on my own. I need a Bible scholar to explain it all to me." This is completely false. Let this sink in: God wants *you* to know Him. When you go to His Word, He wants *you* to understand it. He wants to personally reveal Himself to *you*. Take a look at these two verses from Paul's letter to the Ephesians:

*"I keep asking that the God of our Lord Jesus Christ, the glorious Father, may give you the spirit of wisdom and revelation, so **that you may know** him better. I pray also that the eyes of your heart may be enlightened in order **that you may know** the hope to which he has called you..."*

*- (Eph. 1:17-18a, **emphasis mine**)*

When we rely too heavily on study tools, we miss the opportunity for a personal revelation from our Almighty God.

Throughout the first two or three weeks of Foundation, avoid using extra Bible study tools except when doing a Background Study. (We will talk in detail about Background Studies in the next chapter.) These tools will play an important role a little further into the Bible study process, but if we want to truly fall in love with God's Word, we need to start off by simply soaking in the story. When we go straight to studying the details and relying on others' insights, we run the danger of falling into two traps. First, we can start to see the Bible as simply a textbook we read to get information. Bible reading becomes time spent getting information about God, rather than time spent with God.

A second trap to this approach is that we can give the study tools the same authority we give to Scripture. I once heard someone say, "One thing we must always remember about commentaries: they are simply another Christian's *comments* on Scripture. They are not Scripture themselves." I have a friend who has made a little rule for himself to specifically avoid this second trap. Whenever he is about to grab a commentary, he rereads the passage of Scripture ten times first! This places the Bible verses fresh in his mind before he reads someone else's comments.

Avoiding these traps are not the only reasons to read independently. There are also several blessings when we embrace Independent Reading. First of all, few experiences can compare to the realization that God has just personally revealed a piece of Himself to you. When you are reading along and suddenly find that a passage comes together and makes sense, there can be a tremendous sense of nearness to God. There is also great joy in going to a commentary or hearing a sermon and realizing that God showed you the exact same thing He showed that author or pastor.

You will undoubtedly find that as you read there will be some passages that are difficult to understand. Commentaries can help bring light to some of those passages. Also, there will be times when you will turn to a study tool to find out more information about a person, place, time period etc. (We will talk about that in the section on Background Studies.) But when it comes to Independent Reading, the bottom line is that God wants to spend some time with you. Just the two of you. Take Him up on it. You won't regret it.

Thoughtful Reading

Whenever I discuss Bible reading with people, there is one question that is always met with groans of painful agreement: Do you ever struggle with your mind wandering when you read the Bible? (Maybe you just groaned when you read that question.) The more I talk to people, the more I find this is the most common problem in Bible study.

As we spoke about in the section on Prayerful Reading, the Enemy is specifically working to keep us from focusing on Scripture. In addition to preparatory time spent in prayer, there are some specific steps that we can take as we read to keep this from happening.

First, it takes work to keep our minds from wandering. As we put effort into Thoughtful Reading however, it becomes "built in" to the way we read the Bible. One practice that has helped me focus more than anything else is to read out loud. Have you ever tried reading the Bible out loud? I never did until I had been a Christian for 15 years!

Reading silently, the verses all tend to sound the same – monotone. Reading out loud allows us to hear the emotion in the passage. We can sense the author's compassion, or frustration, or sadness, or joy. We can actually picture the author speaking the passage directly to us. Reading out loud also gives our brains one more way of taking Scripture in, making it that much easier to remember. Study after study shows that – no matter what the information – we remember far more of what we read *and* hear than what we only read.

Another element of Thoughtful Reading is reading from different perspectives. This is most easily done when we keep an underlying question running through our minds as we read. Take Philippians for example. One day you might read Philippians asking: "What would it feel like to be Paul writing this letter?" The next day you could ask: "What would it have been like to sit in the church in Philippi the day this letter was read for the first time?" The third day: "What would my family (or community/country/world) look like if the messages of this letter were lived out in my life and the lives of those around me?"

Develop additional questions that help you focus as you read. We tend to focus more easily and draw more from a passage when we approach it from many different angles, rather than reading it the same way, day in and day out. It is a deception of the Enemy to believe, however subconsciously, that the Bible is a monotone book with nothing new to say to us. Nothing could be further from the truth.

Prayerful Reading, Continuous Reading, Repetitious Reading, Independent Reading, and *Thoughtful Reading.* Utilizing these five techniques will greatly enhance your understanding of, love for, and internalization of God's Word. You will soon find yourself *expecting* the Bible to be the wonderful relationship builder God always intended it to be.

How About A Little Context?

Background Studies

How much thought do you give to the author of a particular book or letter when you are reading the Bible? How about the first readers of that book or letter? Do you put any thought into what they were facing or the surrounding social and political climate? Instinctively we *know* the importance of context in other areas of our lives. For example, the sentence "I'll be back before you know it" carries very different meanings coming from someone who is running to the refrigerator at halftime than if it's coming from your child as she boards a plane bound for her freshman year of college. It is impossible for us to grasp the big picture for any situation or idea unless we first know the context.

Understanding context can make that same kind of difference for studying a book of the Bible. When we begin to learn about such things as the personal details and characteristics of the book's author, the situations and challenges the author and recipients were facing at the time, and the events occurring in the world around them, we gain an entirely new perspective and depth of understanding for the book. Weaving Background Studies into the Foundation Phase provides the necessary context for correctly interpreting and applying a passage to our lives.

There are three basic questions that Background Studies answer:

- *Who* wrote the book? (Author)
- To *Whom* was the book written? (Audience)
- *What* was happening at the time the book was written? (Atmosphere)

Although some of the answers to these questions can be found within the book itself, many times you will need other tools to aid you in your Background Study. Most study Bibles have information at the beginning of each book or in the back of the Bible that provides some context. While this is certainly helpful, I have found that this is rarely all the information I want. At the end of this chapter, you will find a brief guide to some of the tools and resources you may find helpful.

The wonderful thing about Background Studies is that you can dig as deeply as you want to, or simply skim over a few items to bring a general sense of context to the book you are reading. Background Studies should not be done every day. Rather, you may want to set aside three days – one for each Background Study – during your thirty days of Foundation and Framing. (See Appendix A for a suggested timeline.)

If you are not already using one, this is a good time to start a journal or computer file where you can write down the information you discover as you do your Background Studies. If you cannot remember the context you have learned, then you lose the value of ever having learned it. Writing can be one more means of putting something into our brains and helping it to stay there. It also gives us a quick way to refer back to the information. A journal can also go beyond a simple way to track information and become a place where we record those truths God personally reveals to us as we study.

For me, a document on my computer that I can keep adding to works the best. Others have told me that an outline or a narrative journal works better for them. Try a few different options and find the one that helps you organize your information in a way that best helps you to remember – and apply – it.

Background Study 1: Who wrote the book? (*Author*)

Before diving into any external resources, it is always important to start by asking, "What does the Bible have to tell me about the author?" As you read through the book you are studying, start jotting down information about the author. Where was he when he was writing? Is the author one person, or several people writing together? What kind of mood does he appear to be in? Is he encouraging the recipients? Thanking them? Challenging them? Frustrated with them? What other information does he provide that gives you insight into himself?

Only after you have deduced all you can from the book itself is it time to move on to other resources. If you happen to be studying one of Peter's or Paul's letters, you might want to check out the book of Acts for background information. In their letters, Peter and Paul often refer to events that are talked about (some in great detail) in the book of Acts, and Acts is also a good place to gain further insight into James and John, who are also New Testament authors. Obviously the Gospels also contain information about some New Testament authors – particularly those who were among

Jesus' disciples. If you are studying an Old Testament book of the law, you will want to check out Exodus to learn about Moses, or if you are studying David's or Solomon's writings, you will want to read further in Samuel and Kings. Many Study Bibles have a system (called "cross-references") that shows you where in other parts of the Bible you can find information about the passage you are reading.

At this time you can go to any one of your external study tools (Bible dictionaries, handbooks, etc.). Simply look up the author you are studying and read more about him. As you read, write down the key elements you want to remember. This is where you can get creative. You need to find a way of writing this information down so that it will stick with you and make you want to look at it again. My goal is not simply to give you an assignment that you check off the list and leave behind. I want you to fall in love with God's Word and return to your notes over and over again!

I find the easiest way for me to organize my Background Studies is to create a bulleted list with key points at the beginning of my Foundation Outline. (See page 74) You may want to designate a section in your notes to Background Studies. But, as I mentioned earlier, a journal, outline – or something completely different – might work better for you. The key is: Write it down or you won't remember it!

Background Study 2: To Whom is the book written? (*Audience*)

If I wrote a letter to the people in my small group, do you think it would be different from a letter I wrote to everyone in my church? Would a letter to my church be different from a letter to all the Christians in the Seattle area? Would that letter be different from a letter I wrote to every Christian in the United States? The world? The obvious answer is, "Of course they'd be different."

Let me give you three examples of the way these questions apply to various books of the Bible. In II Timothy 1:2 the Apostle Paul says he is writing *"To Timothy, my dear son."* In I Thessalonians 1:1 Paul writes *"To the Church of the Thessalonians."* Peter's first letter is different altogether. I Peter 1:1 has his letter addressed *"To God's elect, strangers in the world, scattered throughout Pontus, Galatia, Cappadocia, Asia and Bithynia..."*

Not only are some books sent to one person and others sent to many, but some are sent to people who are of Jewish background, others sent to Gentiles, and still others sent to both. While we don't need to spend hours and hours studying the recipients (although you can if you like), it certainly helps to understand the author's audience if we are going to fully grasp the purpose of a book.

The methodology of a Background Study on the audience is exactly like that of the Background Study of the author. Start by finding out what you can from the book you are studying, move on to other parts of the Bible (if there are other applicable passages), and then search for information in outside resources. And remember to write it down.

Background Study 3: What was happening at the time it was written? (*Atmosphere*)

If I wrote you a letter about enduring hard times while I sat on the beach in Hawaii, how much clout would I have? Would my "clout level" increase if the letter was written from prison? Of course. Understanding the atmosphere – or setting – for a book is vitally important to understanding the book's message.

The first question to ask is, "When was this book written?" There are a few Biblical books for which scholars are not sure of the actual date of authorship, but for most books they have a relatively good idea as to when a book was written. Most Study Bibles or commentaries will have this information. Establishing the date of authorship can lend tremendous credibility to a book's message. Let's take II Peter as an example. Early on in this letter (verse 16 of chapter 1), Peter writes, "*We did not follow cleverly invented stories when we told you about the power and coming of our Lord Jesus Christ, but we were eyewitnesses of His majesty.*" II Peter was written sometime between 60-70 AD. This means that when Peter wrote these words, there were still many people living who were around when Jesus did all the things Peter was claiming he did. If Peter started fabricating his stories, these "eyewitnesses" could easily have stepped in and pointed out the errancy of his claims. The fact that there were people reading Peter's letter who were also eyewitnesses to the life of Jesus increases the authority of Peter's writing.

After establishing the "when" of a book, the rest of the study on the atmosphere has to do with the situations the authors and recipients found themselves in at the time the book was written. As with any other Background Study, you can be as thorough as you desire. Start with the information you can glean from the Bible itself. Again, Acts can be a good reference for many of the New

Testament letters. If you are studying an Old Testament prophetic book, you will find the historical books (Samuel, Kings, Chronicles, etc.) to be helpful. Similarly, if you're studying an Old Testament history book, the prophetic books can give you insight into the spiritual climate of the time.

For further information, many Bible Dictionaries and commentaries provide background on the issues the authors and recipients were facing. As you read, write some of the key ideas into your Bible study notes. As you gather information from many different sources, having the main points in one location allows for quick, easy review later on.

Many people find that Atmosphere Background Studies can become quite a fascinating exercise. The more you find out about a city, culture, people group, or individual, the more you want to know. There is so much historical information to be found – both Christian and secular – that there is literally almost no end to the depth of study you can do. The key is to find out how much background you need to make the Bible come alive and become more "real" to you. For one person, a 20-minute overview might be plenty. For another, there may not seem to be enough hours in the day.

Study Tools and Resources

Here are some of the tools you might find useful should you choose to dig deeper than the information your Study Bible contains:

Bible Dictionary/Encyclopedia

- Bible Dictionaries and Encyclopedias are extremely useful for researching authors, recipients, and cities.
- There are many good "one-volume" Bible Dictionaries. There are also Bible Encyclopedias that come in several volumes. Some have lots of illustrations and are very easy to use. Others are very thorough and academic in their language. Your best bet is to go to a Christian book store and spend some time leafing through the various choices.

Bible Handbook

- A Bible Handbook explores the customs, politics, and history of various books, cities, and people groups in the Bible, providing a wealth of information for an "atmosphere" Background Study.

Bible Atlas

- A Bible Atlas goes into great depth regarding the geography, climate, landscape, etc. of land regions during Biblical times.
- Note: Basic geographical information can be found in most Bible Dictionaries, Encyclopedias, and Handbooks. The Bible Atlas is a terrific resource for those who are fascinated by geography and want more detailed information as they study a book's atmosphere.

Commentaries

- Commentaries are verse-by-verse or section-by-section discussions of books of the Bible.
- Most commentaries will have some general background

information at the beginning of the chapter pertaining to each book.

- As with many of the other tools mentioned here, commentaries can be found in many different formats – from concise, one-volume commentaries that cover the whole Bible, to complete sets that devote a volume to each book.

- Finally, since commentaries are simply books written by other Christians, every commentary will carry with it the theological positions of its author. You should talk with your pastor or a trusted friend to get a recommendation on which commentary might be best for you.

If you only plan on purchasing one or two of these resources, I would highly recommend a good Bible Encyclopedia and a one-volume commentary of the whole Bible. Most libraries (both church and public) have these resources as well if you do not have the means of obtaining these tools personally.

Many of these resources can also be found on the Internet or through several terrific software programs. This gives you the opportunity to search several books at once, and even "cut-and-paste" information you find into your own Bible study notes. It is also a comparatively inexpensive way to access a vast library of books you might never find at your local Christian bookstore.

Note: For a brief description of several online resources, you can visit the "Resources" link at www.thatyoumayknow.com

WHAT'S THE POINT?

Purpose Statement

A Purpose Statement is simply a short sentence or two that summarizes the central purpose or focus of the book. For an avid reader, a Purpose Statement is the material written on the back cover of a new book. For an executive, it is a company's Mission Statement. For a baseball fan, it is the Box Score of last night's game.

A Purpose Statement helps you to clarify the author's primary theme in your own mind. It will also provide you, later on, with a way to quickly remember what a book of the Bible is about. As you study more and more books of the Bible, it is helpful to have a collection of Purpose Statements as a reminder of which books cover what topics.

The process of developing a good Purpose Statement can be boiled down to four simple steps, woven throughout the Foundation Phase.

Step 1: Read the book at least ten times.

If you have only read a book of the Bible once or twice, you are probably wasting your time to put much effort into developing a Purpose Statement. However, after you have read a book ten times, you will have a pretty good idea about the book's purpose. You just need to put what you know in your head down onto paper.

Step 2: Write a brief summary of what the author is trying to say.

At this point, simply let the thoughts in your mind transfer to paper (or computer file). Write down what you believe to be the author's purpose. Why is he writing this book? Make sure to focus on the overall message rather than the individual concepts and ideas. The over-arching themes in the Bible are just as applicable to our everyday lives as the points made in individual verses.

Don't let yourself get stuck trying to word everything perfectly, and do not worry about getting it all into one or two sentences. That will come later. Of course, if your rough draft is three pages long, you have gone a little overboard. Typically, the rough draft is about a paragraph in length.

Step 3: Read five more days. Then return to the Purpose Statement.

This is very important. Do *not* work on your Purpose Statement everyday. Work on it one day, and then continue with your Repetitious Reading and some of the other Foundation Phase elements for about five days. This goes for almost *every* piece of this Bible study method. I find that most people who have a hard time enjoying Bible study find themselves doing the exact same thing every day. For example, I love pizza, but after a couple days in a row, I want something else. If you focus on different elements on different days, you will find yourself looking forward to returning to each component, rather than feeling like they are just one more thing you have to do.

After reading the book for five more days, read your rough draft and make any corrections you deem necessary. Many of your first impressions will end up in your final draft, so don't feel like you need to do a major overhaul. In fact, you will probably just cut a few things out (because you started out a little too detailed), change a word or two, and that will be it.

Step 4: Repeat and Finalize.

On about Day 20 of your study, repeat Step Three and write a third draft. This may seem like a lot of work, but you will likely find that a majority of the work was done on Day 10. These revisions will usually take you less than five minutes since you are simply refining material that you have already written down.

On Day 25, finalize your Purpose Statement. At this point, your goal is to have the overall purpose of the book condensed into one or two sentences. Since you created your Purpose Statement, you will find that it is easier to remember than if someone else simply told you what the book was about. Below are some examples of Purpose Statements for Romans, II Timothy, and Colossians.

Romans

The universal state of mankind is sinfulness, and righteousness in God's eyes can only come through faith in His sovereign grace, as it is displayed through the life, death, and resurrection of His Son, Jesus Christ. In response to this grace, our lives are to be lived in obedience to God, encouraging others to do the same, so as to bring glory to God.

II Timothy

In the midst of the struggles of living the Christian life, we must continue to develop our passion for Christ and stay focused on God, who is faithful, and whose Word will endure.

Colossians

Christ is the bodily form of God, is supreme over all things, and our fullness is found only in Him. The entirety of our faith, both internal belief and external actions, must be based solely on Christ.

PHASE TWO

Framing

HOLDING IT ALL TOGETHER

Framing

While I watched our house being built, I couldn't help but notice all that hinged on the framing. It only took a week or two to frame the entire house, but the prior work that was done on the foundation and everything that happened afterward was all held together by the framing.

First of all, it was framing that connected everything above ground to everything below ground. Bolts attached the wood to the cement. Metal plates were put in place to keep the house from shifting sideways in the event of an earthquake.

Of equal importance was that the framing was the "hook" all the other elements hung on. It gave each subcontractor a map to follow. The furnace guy knew where to place the ducts and vents so that every room would have heat. The electrician had something to attach wires to so they weren't simply running across the floor or hanging down from the ceiling. The plumber could tell exactly where to put a sink, a toilet, or a shower based on the outline provided by the framing.

Also, the *quality* of the framing is key. To understand the truth of this statement, simply ask someone who hangs sheetrock for a living if he's ever worked on a house that was framed *poorly*. If the framing is done well, everything hangs flush and straight. If it is done poorly, you'll see gaps and cracks appear in no time.

To make sure the framing was done properly, I noticed it was done in two stages. First, there was the framing that followed the outline of the foundation. The framers didn't simply frame one room, move on to the next, build a staircase, add another room, and so on. Rather, they first built the exterior walls and made sure that the overall structure of the house was secure, straight, and solid. Only then did they frame the internal walls, staircases, etc.

Likewise, the Framing Phase of this Bible Study process is made up of two stages:

1. Foundation Outline
   • The "external" walls.
   • Only includes the primary ideas and follows the author's thought process.
   • Very general.
2. Framing Outline
   • The "internal" walls.
   • Breaks the book down further into sections short enough to explore one each day.

Taking the time to "frame" your study of a book or section of the Bible with these two outlines will provide these four benefits:

1. Framing cements in your mind the author's thought process.
2. Framing is the "bridge" that links the general approach of the Foundation Phase with the detailed approach of the Finish Work Phase.

3. Framing gives you a quick way to review a book of the Bible for years to come.

4. Framing breaks down the book you are studying into "day-sized" pieces for deeper study. (Finish Work)

How Can I Follow the Author's Train of Thought?

Foundation Outline[1]

I magine being able to review an entire book of the Bible in the two minutes it takes you to brush your teeth, bring in the mail, pour another cup of coffee, or walk from your office to your car. A Foundation Outline enables you to do just that. Foundation Outlines are comprised of brief phrases that "walk you" through a book of the Bible and help you to understand an author's thought process. This short outline lays out the "foundational" elements of the book in a concise way that cements the Big Picture in your mind.

It would only take you a minute or two at most to read through one of the sample Foundation Outlines at the end of this chapter. Now, if you had been the one to actually create the Foundation Outline, you would not even need to read it. You would know it by heart and could review the key components of a book of the Bible in a very brief time. If you think about it for a moment, I bet you could come up with several more "two-minute windows" in your day. What better use of that time could there be than to meditate on a section of God's Word?

When I discuss outlining in this book, my goal is not to transport you back to high school when you had to completely outline a chapter of your textbook, only to put that outline aside and come up with another detailed outline for the next day's chapter. Rather, my hope is that you will see each element of this process reinforcing, enhancing, and building on what you have done previously. Here is one way to look at it: The Purpose Statement is the title of your outline. The Foundation Outline contains the primary headings – and maybe some sub-headings. (I, II, III & A, B, C) The Framing Outline (see the next chapter) breaks things down a little further. (i, ii, iii) And finally, your notes on paragraphs, words, and phrases add the details. (a, b, c) I can't imagine trying to do all this at once. But if you do a little bit each day, you will soon find that you have a profound understanding of the particular book you're studying – and that you are loving it at the same time!

Before discussing the process of developing a Foundation Outline, it is important to mention that, while outlining in this fashion is helpful for most people, it is not for everyone. Applying the concept of studying from the general ideas to the specific details is the most important thing. If you are more comfortable simply creating a list of general ideas – create a list. If taking the time to write things out in a narrative format is the most enjoyable and effective method for you, then by all means, don't let me steer you away from that. Just make sure that whatever you do, start out by looking at the Big Picture, then the general concepts, and finally, dive into the details. I think you will find that whatever specific *style* you find most useful, applying this *approach* will have immediate – and lasting – rewards.

Developing the Foundation Outline follows the same Four-Step pattern for creating a Purpose Statement that we discussed in the last chapter. (See Appendix A for a timeline of these steps.)

Step 1: Read the book at least ten times.

As with the Purpose Statement, you will end up doing a lot of extra work if you try to create a Foundation Outline when you have only read a book once or twice. Instead, you may try focusing on the Foundation Outline on the day immediately after you worked on the Purpose Statement. Another approach would be to insert a day of Foundational Reading in between the Purpose Statement and Foundation Outline so that you are not doing two "academic" activities on back-to-back days. You just need to find a pattern that works for you and stick to it.

Step 2: Identify the natural breaks and shape them into a rough draft.

While you read, begin to identify the natural breaks in the author's thought process. Where does he change from one topic or story to another? This is not the time to create a heading for every paragraph. As you can see from the examples at the end of this chapter, the entire Foundation Outline will be less than a page, so force yourself to stay general for now.

If you have a Study Bible that already breaks down sections and has headings written in, refrain from using these breaks and headings. There will, of course, be times when the breaks are in exactly the right places, and the headings are worded perfectly. If that's the case, go ahead and use one or two of the headings. However, the headings in most Study Bibles break down the book further than is necessary at this point. Also, give yourself the opportunity to enjoy coming up with phrases that capture the heart of what you believe the author is saying. When you come up with your own headings for your outline, you will enjoy your time in God's Word more, because you will be interacting with God and His Word. You will be a *participant* rather than simply a spectator. Not only that, but you will also remember what you study much better.

Step 3: Read five more days. Then return to your
Foundation Outline.

As I mentioned in the last chapter, it is very important that you not work on the same thing everyday. Put your Foundation Outline away and work on something else (Background Studies or Purpose Statement) or simply read your Bible for a few days. If you created your rough draft on Day 11, plan on editing on about Day 16. Since you are continuing to read the book each day between your edits, you will find at each edit you have a clearer understanding of the book, making your editing more and more simple each time.

To edit your Foundation Outline, read the book again with your rough draft nearby. See if your original choices for primary headings and sub-headings still seem right to you. If so – terrific! If not, make the necessary changes. Most people tend to break things down a little too much in the rough draft. As you read through the book again, you may see that a couple of your headings would fit better under a single heading. At this point, all you want to do is tighten up what you created on Day 11. Remember: You are not reinventing the wheel everyday!

Step 4: Repeat and Finalize

After putting your second draft away and pursuing something else for a few days, you will want to have another quick "editing session" at about Day 21. Each time you edit, you will find fewer and fewer changes need to be made. By Day 26 you will be ready to finalize your Foundation Outline. By now you should have a short (one-half to two-thirds of a page) outline with no more detail than headings and sub-headings. If you have several different levels to your outline, you have actually started to create a Framing Outline, which we will discuss in the next section.

Here are a couple examples of Foundation Outlines:

II Timothy

I. Introduction – 1:1-2

II. Focus on individual faithfulness – 1:3-2:26

    A. Faithfulness of past generations – 1:3-7

    B. Paul's example – 1:8-15

    C. Follow these examples and seek after godliness – 2:1-26

    D. Reminder of God's faithfulness – 2:8-13

III. Warning about the last days – 3:1-9

IV. Paul's Charge – 3:10-4:8

    A. Endure and keep the faith – 3:10-17

    B. Preach the Word – 4:1-8

V. Closing Comments – 4:9-22

    A. Invitation to come to Rome – 4:9-18

    B. Final Greetings – 4:19-22

Colossians

I. Greeting and Introduction – 1:1-2

II. Thankfulness and Prayer for the faith, love, and wisdom of the Colossians – 1:3-14

III. Life must be based on Christ and His supremacy, not the world – 1:15-2:23

    A. Christ is Creator and supreme – 1:15-1:23

    B. Paul's commission to proclaim the mystery of Christ – 1:24-2:5

    C. Life based on Christ rather than the world – 2:6-23

IV. Outward characteristics of a life focused on Christ – 3:1-4:6

    A. Guidelines for personal life – 3:1-17

    B. Guidelines for family and work life – 3:18-4:1

V. Final Greetings – 4:7-18

HOW CAN I BREAK THIS DOWN INTO PIECES I CAN HANDLE?

Framing Outline[1]

†

I have spent many of these pages describing the construction process for our home. Now I want you to take a moment and think back to a time when you watched a house being built in your neighborhood. You remember the process. One day you see a backhoe out there moving dirt around and you can only imagine what the house will look like. A few days later you walk by and see that a foundation has been poured. Over the next few months, you can't wait to see what they get done each day. The frame of the house gives you an idea of what the final shape will be. The walls go up. You see they've decided to go with a tile roof rather than slate. After work one day, you notice that all the builders have gone home, and you sneak in to see what the inside is going to look and "feel" like. (Come on now, I know I'm not the only one who has done this. If they haven't put the doorknobs and locks on yet, I figure they *want* me to take a look.) Finally, they paint the outside, put the finishing touches on the trim, and landscape the yard. Every step of the way, you are more and more interested in seeing what this house is going to be like when it's finished.

On the other hand, if we drive by someone painting a house, putting up siding, landscaping a yard, or installing a window on a house we have *never seen*, we probably won't even slow down. It is when we see something developing from the start that we want to take in every detail.

The same is true with Bible study. Creating an outline, analyzing a paragraph, or looking up the meaning behind a word or phrase is only interesting and valuable when it adds depth and meaning to a book we have started to build a relationship with. It always helps to keep in mind that – unlike most books we read – God wrote His Book for the *very purpose* of strengthening our relationship with Him. Now that's a reason to dig deep!

Developing a Framing Outline is simply the next step in studying from the general to the specific. In Phase One of this book, we discovered how to look at a book as a whole using Foundational Reading, Background Studies, and a Purpose Statement. Most recently, we developed a Foundation Outline. Your Framing Outline will add one or two more "tiers" to the Foundation Outline you already have.

When you are developing a Framing Outline, a good portion of the "work" is done simply by taking out your Foundation Outline. By this point, you have already read the book many times. In a very real way, you already know the material. What you are doing now is *organizing* the material so you will better *remember* it.

As you develop the Framing Outline, you will begin to notice how each paragraph plays into the overall thought process of the author. Later, on days when you are looking at an individual paragraph, phrase, or word, your outline will be an easy reference enabling you to remember where you have come from and where you are going. (If you look at the timeline laid out in Appendix A you will notice that developing a Framing Outline is woven into the four days immediately following the Foundation Phase and leads right into the first day of the Finish Work Phase.)

Since you are now simply organizing something you already know, there is no month-long, four step process of creating and editing your Framing Outline. Rather, there are just a few items to keep in mind that will help streamline the process.

Read One Chapter Each Day

To prepare your Framing Outline, slowly read through the book again with your Foundation Outline in hand. Take it one chapter a day at this point so that you will have the time to read slowly, soaking in all that the author is trying to say.

This is especially true for some of the New Testament letters by Paul, Peter, James, and John. It is important that you allow yourself enough time to truly ponder what is written and follow the author's train of thought. For some of the longer narrative books (e.g. Genesis, the Gospels, Acts), you may decide to take several chapters a day, since you are following a storyline rather than a thought process. Some elements of a story might take an entire chapter in and of themselves (e.g. John 9).

Summarize the Paragraphs

As you read, jot down a word, phrase, or sentence that summarizes each paragraph. If you are studying one of the narrative books of the Bible, you could write a few key phrases that remind you of the major points in each story. This is not the time to ponder every detail of a given paragraph. The purpose for developing a Framing Outline is to show the breakdowns that you will later study in greater depth.

Outlining

As you complete a chapter, formulate the phrases you came up with for your breakdowns into the next tier of your outline. You will typically end up with three to eight phrases for each chapter. I personally do most of my note-taking on a computer, so I simply cut-and-paste the Foundation Outline onto a new page and then add another level. If you handwrite your notes and keep them in a journal, you may want to write your phrases on the same page as your Foundation Outline so they can be reviewed together.

If you remember better in pictures, it might be a good idea to put your Purpose Statement in the middle of a blank sheet of paper, have the primary headings of your Foundation Outline "branch out" from the Purpose Statement, and branch out even further with your new phrases. You could end up with a "visual tree" that represents an entire book on one page.

Whatever you do, be creative! You want your final Framing Outline (whatever that looks like to you) to help you quickly remember what you studied each time you look at it.

The following day, repeat this process for the next chapter. Once you finish the last chapter and have your outline completed, show it to someone. Since your outline is only a page or so, it won't take them more than a couple minutes to read through. Check to see if your reader understands the main points of the book and the way the author moves from one point to the next. This will give you some good input on points that need to be clarified, and you might just hear someone say, "Wow. That sounds like a pretty interesting book. Maybe I should read it myself."

Once you have a complete Framing Outline, and you have

shown it to someone and made any finalizations, you are ready to begin looking at one small section at a time. The paragraph divisions made in your Framing Outline are just the right size to look at one each day without being overwhelmed.

Here are my Framing Outlines for II Timothy and Colossians:

II Timothy

I. Greeting and Introduction – 1:1-2

II. Encouragement to faithful living

    A. Reminder of the faith of Timothy's mother & grandmother – 1:3-5

    B. Encouragement to live faithfully – 1:6-7

    C. Follow Paul's example – 1:8-18

        i. Example of confidence through suffering – 1:8-12

        ii. Example of sound teaching – 1:13-14

        iii. Examples of deserters and faithful friends – 1:15-18

    D. Keep discipling, and persevere – 2:1-7

    E. Stay focused on why we persevere – 2:8-13

    F. Warn others, but focus on your own pursuit of holiness – 2:14-19

    G. Cleanse yourself of all that is unholy – 2:20-21

    H. Flee what is evil, pursue that which is good, being patient and kind – 2:22-26

III. Warning about the last days – 3:1-9

    A. Character traits – 3:1-5

    B. Example – 3:6-9

IV. Paul's Charge – 3:10 – 4:8

    A. All who follow Christ will suffer – Paul as example

B. Endure and focus on the Word

    i. All Scripture is God-breathed and useful for application in all areas

C. Preach the Word – 4:1-2

D. Stay focused – 4:3-5

    i. Many false teachers – 4:3-4

    ii. Keep your head in all situations – 4:5

E. Paul's own example – 4:6-8

    i. The crown of righteousness is in store – 4:8

V. Closing Comments – 4:9-22

A. Invitation to come to Rome – 4:9-13

B. Warning about Alexander – 4:14-15

C. Reaffirmation of God's faithfulness – 4:16-18

VI. Final Greetings – 4:19-22

Colossians

I. Greeting and Introduction – 1:1-2

II. Thankfulness and Prayer for the faith, love, and wisdom of the Colossians – 1:3-14

A. Thankfulness for their faith and love – 1:3-6a

B. Encouragement that the gospel is producing fruit elsewhere as well – 1:6a-8

C. Prayer to God on behalf of the Colossians – 1:9-14

III. Life must be based on Christ and His supremacy, not the world – 1:15-2:23

A. Christ is Creator and supreme – 1:15-1:23

    i. Christ's power and authority over creation – 1:15-20

    ii. Christ's authority over our sin – 1:21-23

B. Paul's commission to proclaim the mystery of
Christ – 1:24-2:5

  i. Paul's commission of service to the church – 1:24-27

  ii. Paul's desire to present everyone perfect in
Christ – 1:28-29

  iii. Paul's purpose is for others to know the mystery of
God – Christ – 2:1-5

C. Life based on Christ rather than the world – 2:6-23

  i. Admonition to remain in Christ rather than return
to the world – 2:6-8

  ii. The work of God/Christ through circumcision,
baptism, and the cross – 2:9-15

  iii. Don't allow others' judgments to sway us from
devotion to Christ – 2:16-23

IV. Outward characteristics of a life focused on Christ – 3:1-4:6

A. Guidelines for personal life – 3:1-17

  i. Setting our hearts and minds on things
above – 3:1-4

  ii. Removing all that belongs to the sinful
nature – 3:5-11

  iii. Replacing those things with godly
characteristics – 3:12-14

  iv. Peace, thankfulness, the indwelling of the Word,
and music – 3:15-17

B. Guidelines for family and work life – 3:18-4:1

C. Request for prayer – 4:2-4

D. Make the most of opportunities with outsiders – 4:5-6

V. Final Greetings – 4:7-18

PHASE THREE

Finish Work

Digging Deep to Discover the Treasures

Finish Work

†

Think of a topic that really fascinates you – maybe a sport, hobby, or intellectual pursuit. One of mine is movies. My wife and I love to go to movies. For me, it doesn't matter if it is a romantic comedy, action flick, or tear-jerking drama. I just thoroughly enjoy getting lost in a well-told story. You know what makes the movie even better? The conversation afterward, when we talk about the different characters, examine the various plot twists, or laugh again as we recall funny lines.

Now, as much as I enjoy talking about and re-living a movie I have seen, being around people who are having a conversation about a movie I have not seen yet isn't nearly as much fun. The parts that are hysterical to them, I can't understand. The intricate twists make no sense since I don't even know the plot.

Finish Work is exactly like the conversation after the movie. It is most fruitful when it is done after Foundation and Framing. During the first two phases we "watched the movie." We followed the storyline. We became familiar with the characters and their unique situations. We established a timeline and put everything in context. We came to an understanding of the emotional tone.

Now the time has come to *explore*. What are the subtle nuances we might have missed? What are the specific applications we can make? Why does the author choose a certain word or phrase to make his point? When you already have a basic understanding of the book you are studying, Finish Work is like building a deeper relationship with an old friend.

The Finish Work Phase of Bible study has five primary benefits:

1. *Finish Work helps you to fall in love with the intricate workings of a book, just as Foundation causes you to fall in love with a book as a whole.*

2. *Finish Work provides a solid, working knowledge of the book. As you connect the elements of Finish Work to the Foundation you already have, you will be depositing the messages of the book into your memory bank – ready to draw on that knowledge whenever you need it.*

3. *Applying the elements of Finish Work to one book will enable you to better understand other portions of Scripture as you study them. God has woven His Word together so that all of the different books support and build upon each other. As you study more and more books, you will find verses from past studies coming to mind to complement the portion of Scripture you are currently studying.*

4. *An in-depth study of the Bible expands the knowledge base from which we share our faith. The more we know the Word, the easier it is for the Holy Spirit to bring the truth to our minds when we are speaking with someone who has questions. Furthermore, as we know **how** to study the Bible and **where** to find information, we are equipped to invite someone else to join us in discovering the answers to their questions.*

5. *Finish Work also prepares our minds for memorization and our hearts for meditation – the core of the internalization process.*

The following chapters will explore the three elements of Finish Work:

- Paragraph Studies
- Word and Phrase Studies
- Life Application

Are you ready to dig deep and discover the treasures waiting in God's Word? The best part is that the treasures in the Bible aren't "hidden treasures." God can't wait to reveal them to you!

I'VE GOT THE BOOK BROKEN DOWN... NOW WHAT DO I DO?

Paragraph Studies[1]

†

Now that you have a Framing Outline, the book of the Bible you are studying is broken down into pieces small enough to carefully examine on a single day. You can now spend time really pondering the stories and messages, while at the same time keeping the overall theme and background information running through your mind. In the Foundation Phase you discovered the context for the book you are studying. With that foundation firmly planted in your mind, you are prepared to study a small portion of Scripture without losing that context.

I have found that the time spent focusing on one or two paragraphs of Scripture have been the most fruitful times of Bible study. Times of meditating on a single idea or thought – while keeping the general purpose in mind – are frequently the times when God has given me the encouragement I needed, corrected a wrong thought or action, or shown me something he wanted me to apply to my everyday life.

Before we begin analyzing a paragraph it is important to identify what type of paragraph we are looking at. Any given book of the Bible typically contains two different types of paragraphs – those paragraphs that tell a story (Historical Paragraphs) or those that explore a concept (Conceptual Paragraphs). Let me give you an example of each.

Historical Paragraph

> "Andrew, Simon Peter's brother, was one of the two who heard what John had said and who had followed Jesus. The first thing Andrew did was to find his brother Simon and tell him, "We have found the Messiah" (that is, the Christ)."
>
> - John 1:40-41

As you can see, the above paragraph is telling a story – or giving a little *history* about Andrew. Many of the Old Testament historical books, as well as the Gospels and Acts in the New Testament, are filled primarily with Historical Paragraphs. In these books, we find story after story about characters young and old, each having their own unique experience with God.

Conceptual Paragraph

> "We proclaim him, admonishing and teaching everyone with all wisdom, so that we may present everyone perfect in Christ. To this end I labor, struggling with all his energy, which so powerfully works in me."
>
> - Colossians 1:28-29

In this paragraph, the Apostle Paul is not so much telling a story as he is making a point. His desire is to have the reader follow his train of thought. He is trying to get across a *concept*. The New Testament letters, as well as the Old Testament poetry and prophecy books, are good examples of books of the Bible consisting largely of Conceptual Paragraphs.

Identifying Historical vs. Conceptual Paragraphs

As you read, ask yourself: "Is the author telling me a story or sharing a concept?" If he is telling you a story, you are reading a Historical Paragraph. If he is sharing a concept, it is a Conceptual Paragraph. Once you have identified which type of paragraph you are reading, you can use the appropriate approach to analyze that paragraph.

Paragraph Summary (Historical Paragraphs)

A Paragraph Summary is very similar to a miniature Background Study. Approach Historical Paragraphs as an investigative reporter would - ask the Five W's and an H: Who? What? Where? When? Why? and How?[2] Of course not every paragraph will answer all six questions, but these questions provide a good starting point as you read and reread the paragraph.

At this point, it is important to organize this information in a way that suits your own personal style of learning. As I mentioned earlier, I like to use an outline format because I find it quick and simple, and it enables me to continually break down the book until I end up with one long outline containing all of my notes. If this works for you – terrific! Many people reading this book, however, will learn much better by journaling, writing a song, or drawing a picture. Find a way that helps you understand the story better and remember it more thoroughly. Then dive right in.

The purpose of writing a Paragraph Summary is to spend enough time in a paragraph that you can ponder the events and put yourself into the story. The more you begin to understand the events, characters, and surroundings, the more you will begin to think of these stories as your own.

Let's take another look at the paragraph from John 1:40-41 and two ways we might organize a Paragraph Summary.

> *"Andrew, Simon Peter's brother, was one of the two who heard what John had said and who had followed Jesus. The first thing Andrew did was to find his brother Simon and tell him, "We have found the Messiah" (that is, the Christ)."*
>
> - John 1:40-41

Outline Format

I. Andrew

    A. Simon's brother

    B. John's disciple

    C. Followed Jesus

        i. Went immediately and told Simon, "We have found the Messiah."

Journal Format

Andrew was one of John the Baptist's early disciples. When he heard what John had to say about Jesus, he followed Him. Andrew was also Simon Peter's brother. After spending some time with Jesus, Andrew went right away to Simon Peter and told him, "We have found the Messiah." Messiah is another word for "Christ."

Paragraph Map (Conceptual Paragraphs)

When studying a Conceptual Paragraph, one of the most useful tools for effectively understanding and remembering the paragraph is the Paragraph Map. One day while reading one of Paul's letters, I realized that he had written an entire paragraph with one sentence - lots of commas and only one period. I thought, "Which phrase refers to which other phrase? I need a map to navigate this paragraph!" So I developed one. I read through the paragraph again and again until I was able to see how Paul was developing his thought process. Since that time, I have found it an extremely helpful tool when analyzing Conceptual Paragraphs. Not only will a Paragraph Map help you identify the author's thought process, but it will also clarify key ideas and points and will show the relationship between the main points and the secondary points or phrases.

As with the Paragraph Summary, the Paragraph Map begins as you slowly read and reread a paragraph. As you do, identify what the author is saying and how he is using each phrase to say it.

This is an excellent time to explore the ways that other translations phrase the same paragraph. Reading the passage in another translation will almost always result in a better understanding of the passage and the author's thought process. Since we are only talking about a paragraph – maybe two – at this point, it is well worth the extra two to four minutes it takes to read those paragraphs in a few other translations. (Note: If you do not have more than one Bible and would like to compare multiple translations, there are several tools in print and on the Internet to help you do that. Visit your local Christian bookstore, search the Internet, or go to the Resources page of *www.thatyoumayknow.com* to get pointed in the right direction.)

Once again, a Paragraph Map can be done as an outline, journal entry, or any other way you find helps you understand and remember the passage. Now we will return to Colossians 1:28-29 and see how a Paragraph Map can be used to analyze a passage.

"We proclaim him, admonishing and teaching everyone with all wisdom, so that we may present everyone perfect in Christ. To this end I labor, struggling with all his energy, which so powerfully works in me."

- Colossians 1:28-29

Outline Format

    I. We proclaim Him (Christ)

        A. How?

            i. Admonishing

            ii. Teaching

                a. With all wisdom

        B. Why?

            i. So that we may present everyone perfect in Christ

                a. To this end I labor

                        (a) Struggling with all His energy

                            (i) Powerfully works in me

Journal Format

Paul's desire is clear – to proclaim Christ. He proclaims Christ both by admonishing/encouraging and instructing/teaching. Paul wants to make sure that his admonishment and teaching is not just from his own ideas, but with wisdom. Paul also has a clear purpose for his proclaiming of Christ: he wants to present everyone perfect in Christ. That is the desired end result of all his struggles. Finally, he recognizes that he is not struggling under his own power, but by the indwelling, powerful Spirit of Christ.

As I mentioned at the outset of this chapter, Paragraph Summaries and Paragraph Maps will prove to be some of the most fruitful elements of your study of a book. Just as it was important early on to get an overview of a book by reading it in its entirety, it is equally important now to read slowly, anticipating that God's desire is to reveal His will and His Word to you. You will come to a greater understanding of the passage as well as a deep love for God and His beautifully woven Word.

CAN I REALLY LEARN ANYTHING FROM ONE WORD?

Word and Phrase Studies

I love baseball. I love almost everything about baseball. I could do without the politics of professional baseball, but the game...ah the game. Now I must admit I haven't always loved baseball. I used to see a game on TV and think, "Why would anyone watch a baseball game? It's so boring." If you just nodded your head in agreement – I understand. As much as I love baseball, I completely understand why some people don't.

Baseball is a game where the beauty is found in the details. Most people prefer football and basketball because of the high scores, continuous movement, and flashy plays. After all, even a grand slam, an over-the-wall catch, or a stolen base only lasts a few seconds. It is what happens in between pitches, catches, and hits that makes baseball terrific. (You "non-baseball" people, please bear with me for just a few more sentences.)

If you talk at length to any true baseball fan, you will find yourself in a conversation about what pitch to throw and when, which players can hit a curve ball, why the coach went with the right-handed relief pitcher instead of the southpaw. Every baseball conversation eventually comes around to a conversation about the details. That is why so many people find baseball boring. If you are not willing to dive in, you will never quite "get it." When you look at baseball only in general terms – nine guys standing around a whole lot in between pitches and hits – you miss the beauty that lies below the surface.

The fantastic thing about the Bible is that the Bible's beauty is found in the general and the specific. As we saw in the section on Foundation, simply reading a book of the Bible to get an overview can be very enjoyable and meaningful. However, there is also much treasure to be found in the specific words and phrases of Scripture.

Over the years, Word Studies have added great depth to my study of any book. I have also found that Word Studies are best done in the midst of exploring paragraphs and making life application, rather than in large groups all at once. If Word Studies are used as "seasoning" to your study they will provide great insight and knowledge. But just as too much seasoning can mask – rather than enhance – a food's true flavor, trying to do too many Word Studies in one sitting can become overwhelming and tedious. (NOTE: In the 60-Day Adventure in Philippians found in Appendix A, notice that you will never do more than one Word Study on any given day.)

By the time you finish your study of a particular book, you will have a handful of Word Studies on note cards, throughout your outline, within your journal entries, or however else you choose to organize your thoughts. These Word Studies will become yet another way to augment your understanding of God's Word.

How do I decide which words or phrases to study?

As you read slowly through a passage of Scripture take note of those words or phrases that seem central to the message of that paragraph. If a word or phrase is *repeated*, this is a perfect one to pick for your next Word Study. It may also be helpful to study words and phrases that you are unfamiliar with. By this time in your study of a book of the Bible, you will already know the book quite well, and the main words and phrases will most likely be very easy for you to spot.

Two Types of Words

Just as we talked about two types of paragraphs in the previous chapter (Historical and Conceptual), there are also two different types of words or phrases: Topical and Conceptual.

Topical words are concrete words that represent people, places, events, etc. Topical words cause you to ask questions such as: Who was this person? Where was this city and how big was it? What was this event all about? What was this item used for?

Conceptual words are more abstract, and – as the name suggests – they convey concepts or ideas. Conceptual words lead us to questions like: What is the author trying to communicate by using this word or phrase? How would someone who spoke the original language have understood this word? How is this phrase used or translated in other parts of the Bible? Below are some examples of each:

Topical Words

Ephesus	Cross
Drink Offering	Cubit
Roman Prison	Tychicus
Passover Feast	Holiest of Holies
Barnabas	Ceremonial Washing

Conceptual Words

Fullness	False Humility
Patience	Hallowed
Holiness	Set Your Minds
Apostle	Faithful
Be Transformed	Sanctified

It is important to identify the type of word or phrase you are looking at because the Bible study tools used to research each type differ from each other. Let me reassure you that once you have done one or two Word Studies, you will find that the process is quite simple and that it adds tremendous insight into the passage you are studying.

Tools Needed for Word Studies

Bible

It is important to have a Bible that is a standard translation (New International Version, New American Standard, King James Version, etc). Recently, there have been several good Bible paraphrases written in contemporary language (e.g. The Message). While these Bibles certainly have many good purposes, they are not the best to use for Word Studies as most study tools are linked to particular translations rather than the contemporary paraphrases.

Exhaustive Concordance

An Exhaustive Concordance provides *every* instance of *every* word in the Bible. For example, you can look up the word *love* in an Exhaustive Concordance and you will find every verse in the Bible that uses the word *love*. Each Exhaustive Concordance is linked to a specific translation of the Bible (e.g. *The NIV Exhaustive Concordance* is linked to the New International Version of the Bible). Make sure the Exhaustive Concordance you purchase is linked to the Bible translation you own.

Expository Dictionary

In many instances, two or more Greek or Hebrew words are translated into the same English word in your Bible. For example, the Greek words *agape, phileo,* and *eros* are all translated "love" in English. However, these words all have subtle meanings that make them quite different. An Expository Dictionary will allow you to look up the English word and see the various Greek or Hebrew words and their differences.

Bible Dictionary/Encyclopedia

These can be found in a single volume or a multi-volume set. You use these in exactly the same way you would use an encyclopedia to find background on people, places, events, etc.

All of these resources can also be found on the Internet or purchased as computer software. Many times, you can purchase one piece of software that will come with several different Bible translations, Bible Dictionaries, Expository Dictionaries, and an Exhaustive Concordance. This will give you a vast library of books at a cost much lower than buying even a handful of the books individually.

The Three "R's" of a Good Word Study

An effective Word Study will have three basic components: *Read*, *Research*, and *Return*.

Read

The first thing to do is to read the word or phrase in the context it is written and see how much this alone tells you about the word's meaning. As you move to the next component – Research – make sure you keep your Bible open and the passage handy.

Research

The Research element of a Word Study varies depending on whether you are studying a Topical Word or a Conceptual Word. For a Topical Word Study, the research starts with looking up the word in a Bible Dictionary/Encyclopedia (not an Expository Dictionary). Once you have done that, read through the article and jot down any notes that will help you remember the main elements of that word or phrase. For example, if you are looking up a city, you will want to take note of where the city was located, its size, and any significant events that may have occurred there.

For a Conceptual Word Study, you will want to use an Expository Dictionary. As I mentioned earlier, sometimes there are multiple Greek or Hebrew words translated into the same English word. If you look up your word in an Expository Dictionary and notice there are multiple Greek or Hebrew words, how do you know which one is "your" word? This is where the Exhaustive Concordance comes in.

Every Exhaustive Concordance has a numbering system in which each number corresponds to only one Greek or Hebrew word. Each Exhaustive Concordance is slightly different, but typically, the main pages of an Exhaustive Concordance will have three columns. The first will give the reference for the verse. The second column will include part of the verse, and the third column will have the corresponding number. Let's look at an example from the New International Version for two instances where the word *love* is used.

Example of Exhaustive Concordance Layout

| John 11:3 | *"Lord, the one you **love** is sick."* | 5797 |
| John 13:34 | *"...**Love** one another."* | 26 |

If you were studying John 13 and decided to do a Word Study on *love*, you would look up this passage in the Exhaustive Concordance and take note of the number "26." At this point, you would simply look in the back of the concordance (where all the numbers and their Greek/Hebrew words are listed) and notice that the number 26 corresponds to the Greek word *agape*. Taking a minute to do this will allow you to go straight to the entry for *agape* in your Expository Dictionary rather than wading through all the entries for the word *love*. Once you have found the correct word in your Expository Dictionary, jot down the meaning of the word as well as any added insight the Expository Dictionary has provided.

The Exhaustive Concordance can also be useful for comparing different verses in the Bible where the same Greek or Hebrew word is used. For example, let's say we were doing a Word Study on the word *humility* from James 3:13 *"Who is wise and understanding among you? Let him show it by his good life, by deeds done in the **humility** that comes from wisdom."* If we looked in our Exhaustive Concordance, we would find that the Greek word *prautes* is only translated "humility" one other time in the Bible. However, we would also see that the same word is translated "gentleness, gentle, gently, humbly, and meekness." Depending on how much time we had, we could look at these different passages and gain further understanding of the word *prautes* and the ways it was used by people who spoke Greek as their native tongue.

Return

Finally, it is always crucial to Return to the passage whenever you finish a Word Study. After all, the purpose of a Word Study is to help you further comprehend the passage you are studying, not to simply be an academic exercise to complete. Take a few minutes to reread the passage, keeping in mind any new insights you gained from your Word Study. You may want to include these insights in a journal or other method of reflection you use.

Organizing Your Word Studies

In order to remember and access the information you have learned in your Word Study, you will want to write it down and organize it. Following are several different options you could explore.

Card File

This may sound old-fashioned, but the card file may well be the easiest and most useful method for organizing Word Studies. All you need is a pack of 3x5 cards and a recipe box. Whenever you do a Word Study, simply jot your notes on one of the cards and put it in your box. Over the years, your box will fill up and you will be able to return to it whenever you come across a word that you think you may have studied previously.

I find that most people choose to organize their card files alphabetically. However, some might choose to put in a little extra time and separate their Topical words from Conceptual words, or separate the card file with dividers marking categories. I would recommend that you start alphabetically and add only those extra steps that *enhance* your Bible study time.

Computer File

If you do most of your Bible study note-taking on your computer, you might want to create a computerized version of the card file. The greatest benefit of keeping a card file on your computer is that you can continually add more information without trying to fit it onto a small card.

You can also link your computer file to other documents on your computer or websites you discovered while researching your word. As the Internet becomes more and more integrated into the way we use our computers, the opportunities to link vast amounts of information will only increase and become easier.

Within Your Final Outline

Let me warn you upfront: This is the most time-consuming method. However, if you do much *teaching* of the information you study, this is a very helpful tool. I am often asked to teach on a specific section of Scripture and if this is a section I have already studied, I know that all my notes – from Background Studies to Word Studies – are all together in one place. It takes me longer to study and organize my notes than it would for most people, but when it comes time to prepare to teach, it sure is useful to have all the information already organized. If you are a pastor, Sunday school teacher, or Bible teacher of some sort, you might want to give this a try.

As I close this chapter, let me remind you that the most important thing to keep in mind as you add Word Studies to your time in the Bible is that Word Studies are meant to enhance your enjoyment and knowledge, not become drudgery. Word Studies are one part of the Bible study process you can spend hours on – or minutes.

Returning to my baseball analogy, a basic understanding of some of the strategy (details) of baseball will increase almost anyone's experience of the game. However, as much as I love baseball, I definitely know a few people who are so into the details, I simply cannot keep up. They love to talk for hours about every detail of a player who lived four decades ago. I would say I am somewhere in the middle.

When it comes to Word Studies, I have found that there is a continuum of enjoyment and effectiveness. Almost everyone will find it helpful to add at least a handful of Word Studies to a book of the Bible they are studying. Others will find great value in spending hours researching one word or phrase. Most will find themselves somewhere in the middle.

Let me suggest you try a few Word Studies with the next book you study. If you find yourself truly benefiting from your Word Studies, add a few more to your daily times in God's Word. On the other hand, if you come to see Word Studies as a tedious exercise that bears little fruit, then only do Word Studies for primary phrases and the words you do not understand. Whether you do many Word Studies or only a handful, you will likely find that they greatly increase your comprehension, and therefore your enjoyment, of God's Word.

HOW DOES THIS APPLY TO MY LIFE?

Life Application

†

Why do we study the Bible? Do we do it because we are supposed to? Because God is going to be angry or disappointed if we don't? Because it's a habit?

Let's take one more look at the very first lesson in the Setting the Stage section of this book:

To truly love God with our whole being, we must integrate the Word into every area of our lives.

The primary reason we spend time in God's Word is that we love Him and want Him to use our time in the Bible to make us more like Him. He wants to encourage us in our everyday lives. He desires to challenge us in areas where we need to grow. He wants to show us how to use our gifts to share Him with others. He uses His Word to give us guidelines for living "life to the full." (John 10:10) Bottom line: God's desire is that His Word would be practical and applied.

If we are gaining head-knowledge about God, but not actually becoming more like Him, have we really accomplished all that God has for us? Of course not. God wants so much more for us than we ever want for ourselves. If we leave out Life Application – the final step in the Bible study process – then we have really missed the whole point. However, as we apply God's Word to our everyday lives, we will be changed. We will see just how useful and relevant the Bible is – today!

While we are taking a look at Life Application as a final step in the process, this does not mean it is only done in the last few days of study. We can – and must – make application all throughout our study. During the Foundation Phase, you will surely identify some overarching principles you can apply. Similarly, there will be points of application as you look at specific stories, paragraphs, or even an individual word or phrase. God's Word – general ideas and specific commands – is meant to be applied.

Life Application is comprised of two basic steps. First – identify the *Principle* in the passage you are studying. Second – take *Action*. Let's take a look at these one at a time.

Principle

prin·ci·ple (prîn_se-pel) *noun*

1. A basic truth, law, or assumption: *the principles of democracy.*

2. **a.** A rule or standard, especially of good behavior: *a man of principle.* **b.** The collectivity of moral or ethical standards or judgments: *a decision based on principle rather than expediency.*[1]

Life Application begins by identifying the principle. The above definition reminds us that a principle is very basic. We can often make the Bible more difficult to understand than it really is. There are certainly some difficult passages in the Bible. However, many portions of Scripture have one main point God is communicating.

Our task here is to identify that main point.

By this stage in your Bible study, your mind is already prepared to easily identify the principle. You have already read and reread the passage, created background notes, written theme statements, developed outlines, analyzed paragraphs, and dug deep into word studies. To identify the principle, simply take the knowledge you already have and read the Scripture while asking the following question: *What is the basic truth, rule, or standard in this passage?*

As you identify the principle, there are a couple of things to keep in mind. First of all, there may be secondary principles within the context of the passage you are studying. For example, in the fourth chapter of Philippians, Paul's primary message is one of partnering with others in ministry – specifically in the area of financial partnership. However, it is clear that within that context one could find secondary principles of contentment, thankfulness, and recognition that God is the Great Supplier.

As you seek to apply a passage, ask God to reveal what it is that He wants you to apply. At one point in your life, you may read Chapter Four of Philippians and feel God calling you to be content with your present situation. At another time, you might read the same passage and feel God encouraging you to support another ministry with your finances. This is why it is so important to continually invite the Holy Spirit to guide your time in the Word. He needs to identify what you need to apply. He needs to reveal His Word to you. He must be present with you for the Bible to make the life-changing impact He desires for you.

Finally, remember that you are not out to create a whole new outline at this point. This is the time to ponder and meditate on God's Word. A key part of identifying a principle is putting your pen down – or sliding away from your computer – and *listening*.

Action

ac·tion (àk_shen) *noun*

1. The state or process of acting or doing.
2. A deed
3. A movement or a series of movements.[2]

In the first chapter of the Book of James, we read, *"But be **doers** of the Word, and not hearers only..."* (Verse 22, NKJV, emphasis mine) Action is the "doing" part of the Bible study process. As you identify the principles in Scripture you will begin to see how they might be applied. However, it is when you take specific action on those principles that you will finally see how *practical* Life Application really is.

I don't know about you, but I often find that after I put my Bible down, I can go through the rest of my day without ever thinking about – let alone applying – what I have read. It is relatively easy while I am still in my time of prayer and study to see the application I need to make. It is an entirely different matter to put these principles into practice as I go through the activities and distractions of my day. All too often I leave out the *action* part of my Bible study.

For all of us, taking action needs to become the natural response when we recognize a biblical principle. When you identify a principle that God wants you to apply, develop an "action plan" and write it down right away. I cannot emphasize enough how important it is to *write your action steps down*. We can all have good intentions about putting principles into action. But we also have many things that cloud our memories when it comes to actually carrying out those intentions. Writing down your action steps will likely prove to be the single most helpful tool if you truly desire to implement the principles you identify in Scripture.

When it comes to developing action steps, there are three crucial characteristics to keep in mind: actions are *specific, measurable*, and *visible*. For example, in Ephesians 5:25 we read, "*Husbands, love your wives, as Christ loved the Church and gave himself up for her...*" While loving my wife is the principle in the passage, writing down "I need to love Kari more" is completely insufficient. How do I know if I am actually improving? How do I know if I ever accomplish this action?

If I am going to take this principle and turn it into an action, I need to put some specific, measurable guidelines on this action. The more specific and measurable my actions are, the more likely it is that I will actually do them. If I change "I need to love Kari more" into "I need to have a regular date night and bring her flowers more often," I am headed in the right direction. In fact, I should get even more specific than that. My action plan could read, "In order to show my love to Kari more, I will schedule a date night – just the two of us – once every other week, and I will bring her flowers at least once each month." Now that is some life application! Later, I can look back and see where I have succeeded and where I could improve.

Finally, it is vitally important to keep your action steps where you will be reminded of them. Actions must be visible to be effective. If you only see them when you are actually reading your Bible, the chances of remembering them in the midst of meetings, children, errands and projects are pretty slim. Find a way to keep your action steps in front of you. That might mean putting a sticky note on the bathroom mirror, your desk at work, or the dashboard of your car. I frequently look at my computerized calendar, with my to-do list right on the side of the screen. I have started putting my action steps right into my to-do list along with phone calls to set up, projects to work on, and events to schedule. You need to find a system that will work for you – and then put it into practice.

I pray that you will develop two habits in the coming months. One – that you would regularly listen to God as He reveals the principles in His Word to you. And two – that you would work out a plan for turning those principles into specific, measurable, visible actions. Developing these two habits will put you in a position where God can – and will – mold you into the person He desires you to be.

THE NEXT STEP

Internalization

HIDING GOD'S WORD IN YOUR HEART

Internalization

W hat do you think of when you hear the word "memorize?" I find that for most people, it seems to make
them cringe. When I hear the word "memorize," the
phrase that immediately comes to mind is "from the neck up."
Memorization seems to imply sticking something in your brain and
hoping it will not go away. Not exactly the way we want to think
of the Bible.

Almost every time I teach a *Falling in Love with God's Word
Workshop*, I ask the participants, "How many of you have ever tried
to memorize Scripture?" Almost every hand goes up. I follow that
question up with, "How many of you have quit?" Even more hands
go up. (I'm still trying to figure that one out.)

In truth, God does not want us to simply attempt to place more
Scripture in our heads, but to *internalize* it. He wants the Bible to
be a part of us. He wants us to carry it with us all day – every day.
He wants us to be in relationship with Him through His Word. He
wants His Word to be as real and alive to us today as it was to the
people He inspired to pen the words in the first place.

The process of Scripture Internalization is two-fold. The first
level is simply built-in to this entire Bible study process. If you
apply this process to any book of the Bible, you will come to the
end knowing that book better than any other you have ever studied. Portions of it you will know word-for-word. The second level

of internalization is for those who desire to know even more of the book – maybe even all of it – word-for-word. The remainder of this section explores how we approach this second level.

This second level of internalization plays out differently from person to person. We all learn at different speeds and in various ways. While I have provided a daily guide for applying the entire Bible study process, this second level of internalization cannot be fit into the same time frame.

My purpose in the pages that follow is to give you practical tools you can use – both within the 60-day Adventure and beyond – to help you internalize to whatever level you desire. Whether you choose some key verses to internalize or decide to tackle a whole book, these tools will help you accomplish your goal.

Make sure you keep this in mind whenever you think about internalizing Scripture: *The goal should always be to know the Word, not just the words.* This is the heart of internalization. When we seek to simply know the words, we are selling the Bible short. However, when learning the words becomes an enhancement of our knowledge of the Bible's Author, we will find ourselves loving God and His Word more deeply than ever before.

WHY SHOULD I INTERNALIZE SCRIPTURE?

Five Reasons

I f you have already read most of this book – and possibly even completed the first thirty days of the 60-Day Adventure in Philippians (see Appendix A) – then you already know that internalization can be "built in" to the way we study the Bible. However, if you turned right to this section hoping for some quick "Scripture memory techniques," let me encourage you to read this chapter carefully, and discover how *internalization* is very different from – and much more effective than – *memorization*. I have found five different reasons for all of us to integrate Scripture Internalization into the way we study our Bibles.

God Commands Us To

Much of the first section of this book was dedicated to this idea. We spent several pages looking at verses such as Deuteronomy 6:4-9 (*"These Commandments I give you today are to be upon your hearts…"*), Psalm 119:9-16 (*"I have hidden Your Word in my heart that I might not sin against you."*), and Colossians 3:16-17 (*"Let the Word of Christ dwell in you richly…"*). All throughout the Bible we find passages encouraging – and commanding – us to know the Bible in such a way that we carry it with us throughout our day.

I have known these verses for a very long time, but only in the last ten years or so have I actually put them into practice. I spent many years trying to fill my head with knowledge about the Bible.

I spent very little time actually saturating my mind *with* the Bible. As you begin this journey of internalizing Scripture, let me warn you that once you begin to write God's Word upon your heart, hide His Word in your heart, and let His Word dwell in you richly, you will be hooked! I have found that every book I internalize makes me want to internalize more.

Internalizing Scripture is Encouraging

I vividly remember the first time I realized I had internalized – rather than memorized – Scripture. It was late in the summer of 1993 and I had been reading Philippians every day for a little over a month. I was driving down Interstate 5 in Tacoma, Washington, thinking about Philippians and I began to realize that I knew some sections of it by heart. At that point, all I had been doing was reading and studying the background of the book.

It was so uplifting to have the words of the Bible at the forefront of my mind. I found myself thinking about Philippians at times other than my "study time." As I drove, walked, relaxed, and ran errands I found that I was *meditating* on God's Word. I believe God wants to remind us of His promises, faithfulness, goodness, and love for us as we walk through the joys and challenges of each day.

The Bible is Useful

Most people do not believe this statement. They believe the Bible was written *to* people 2000 years ago, *by* people 2000 years ago, and *for* a society that existed 2000 years ago. Not many people come right out and say that, but the way we live our lives reveals it to be true.

Take a look at the third chapter of II Timothy. Paul starts out with these words: *"But mark this: there will be terrible times in the last days..."* He goes on to describe what society will look like.

"People will be lovers of themselves, lovers of money, boastful, proud, abusive, disobedient to their parents, ungrateful, unholy, without love, unforgiving, slanderous, without self-control, brutal, not lovers of the good, treacherous, rash, conceited, lovers of pleasure rather than lovers of God – having a form of godliness but denying its power."

- II Timothy 3:2-5

Does that sound like a 2000 year-old society that has long since passed away, or does that describe a society you experience everyday? I know that in my community, I don't have to look very far – sometimes only in the mirror – to find people who possess these traits. After going into a little more detail about society and about his own life, he wraps up this chapter with the following words:

*"...You have known the Holy Scriptures, which are able to make you wise for salvation through faith in Christ Jesus. All Scripture is God-breathed and is **useful** for teaching, rebuking, correcting and training in righteousness, so that the man of God may be thoroughly equipped for every good work."*

- II Timothy 3:15-17, **(emphasis mine)**

Paul was saying that Scripture is a useful tool for someone who lives in a society like the one he described earlier. Whenever I can look at my society and see that the first half of II Timothy Three no longer applies, then – and only then – can I possibly entertain the thought that the last half of the chapter no longer applies.

In Ephesians Six, Paul writes of the spiritual battle every Christian is engaged in. He also states that God has given us His Word as a sword – the only *offensive* weapon mentioned. If we are going into battle, shouldn't we carry the biggest, most useful sword possible? The more Scripture we know, the more the Holy Spirit can bring it to mind at times when it can help us. Those may be times of temptation when we need a reminder, times of sadness when we need encouragement, or opportunities to share our faith when we need boldness. It is far more likely that the Holy Spirit will bring Scripture to our minds if we have done the work to put it there in the first place.

Internalized Scripture is a Wonderful Ministry Tool

This point can best be illustrated with a true story. When I was preparing the Gospel of John for the stage, back in 1995, I had hired a director who lived in Seattle. He would come down to Tacoma Monday through Wednesday, and I would go to Seattle on Fridays and Saturdays. On one return trip to Tacoma, I did something many people consider a big no-no: I picked up a hitch-hiker. After tossing his backpack in the back seat, he hopped in the front, introduced himself (his name was Anthony), and off we went.

I started off the hour-long trip by asking where he was heading. "Just traveling. Sort of finding myself," was his reply. Not too much time passed before he asked me what I did. I told him that I was a youth and worship pastor and that I was working on a one-man dramatization of the Gospel of John. I should tell you that the typical response to telling someone you are "in ministry" is either dead silence or extreme interest. Anthony seemed very intrigued – so much so that he asked me to tell him some of the stories. While I didn't sit and quote word-for-word, we did spend the final half of the trip telling stories and talking about different people in the Gospel of John.

As I pulled over to the side of the highway in Tacoma, I asked him if he had a Bible. He said, "No." I asked if he'd like one. (I have a small one I always keep in the armrest of the car for those Seattle traffic jams.) He replied, "Totally! I completely forgot to bring anything to read. I'd love it!" As I handed him a Bible and he stepped out of the car, I posed one last question. "Anthony, would you mind if I prayed for you and your trip?" Without saying a word, he dropped his knees to the pavement, folded his hands, and bowed his head in the passenger seat. As I placed my hand on his shoulder and prayed, I must admit that I was only partly thinking about the prayer. The other part of me was wondering if all the people driving by were thinking that I had him down on his knees with a gun to his head. I was just waiting for sirens and flashing lights.

My prayer was short, we said our "good-byes," and I drove off. I have no idea where Anthony is today, or whether he ever read that Bible. However, I do remember God's promise in Isaiah 55:11, *"…So is my Word that goes out from my mouth: it will not return to me empty, but will accomplish what I desire and achieve the purpose for which I sent it."* I am convinced that – at the very least – God used

His Word that day as a seed planted on fertile soil.

Many Christians feel they do not know the Bible well enough to adequately share their faith. As I rode down the street with Anthony, we never talked theology. I never felt like I had to quote verses from all over the Bible. In fact, I think that would have hindered things. I do believe that the more Scripture we internalize, the more God will use His Word to transform *us*. As we become more like Him, conversations about God will become a natural outflow of the way we live our lives. Sometimes, we will share a lot of Scripture. Other times, we'll take a drive, tell a few stories, and say a prayer.

You Will Never Be Without Your Bible

I am not going to get into a big "end times" discussion here, but I do know there are many people who believe that the day could come when Bibles will not be as readily available as they are today. In many areas of the world, that day is already here! We cannot know when the same thing could happen to us. If that day ever comes for me, I do not want to be without God's Word.

Several years ago, I was teaching a *Falling in Love with God's Word Workshop* and discussing this very point. One woman raised her hand and stated, "If they ever take away our Bibles and lock us up, I want to be in the cell next to you." The class erupted with sounds of laughter and nods of agreement, but I quickly responded, "I don't want that kind of pressure!" As I pointed to various people around the room, I continued, "I may know John, but how about you learn Matthew, you learn Romans, you learn Ephesians, you learn some Psalms, you learn First Corinthians…" Wouldn't that be so much better?

This concept goes far beyond times of persecution however, and applies directly to any point in your day when your Bible is not open in front of you. Internalization provides us with a constant awareness of those things that are on the heart of God.

✝

As we come to the end of this chapter, consider this quote from Chuck Swindoll, well-known author, speaker, pastor, and chancellor of Dallas Theological Seminary.

> *"I know of no other single practice in the Christian life more rewarding, practically speaking, than memorizing Scripture...No other single exercise pays greater spiritual dividends! Your prayer life will be strengthened. Your witnessing will be sharper and much more effective. Your attitudes and outlook will begin to change. Your mind will become alert and observant. Your confidence and assurance will be enhanced. Your faith will be solidified."*[1]

We *need* to internalize God's Word. It needs to become a part of us because God tells us we need it. It is encouraging. It is useful. It is a wonderful ministry tool. And there are many times when you do not have your Bible with you. If you have internalized it – you will *always* have it with you.

Is there Anything I Shouldn't Do When I Am Internalizing Scripture?

Three Don'ts

†

I have spent most of this book encouraging you to incorporate various practices that will integrate Scripture Internalization into your study of the Bible. There are, however three "don'ts" of Scripture Internalization.

Don't Forget the Message

Sometimes it is easy to become so focused on getting the words in the right order, that we forget the point of the passage. Always remember: *The goal is to know the Word, not just the words.* It is vitally important to work at keeping the message fresh.

One way to accomplish this is to keep the *emotion* in the passage as you internalize. Continue to read out loud, and see and hear the characters speaking and interacting. It is very easy to bear down on the words and allow them to become void of emotion. Avoid this at all costs! The more alive the Living Word is to you, the easier it will be to remember the words.

Another tool for keeping the message fresh is to make sure that every week or so you take a break from the detail-oriented nature of Scripture Internalization (and Finish Work for that matter) and spend a day going back to Foundational Reading. Taking a day away from the process of internalization to simply enjoy the story or letter makes it much easier to internalize when you come back to it the following day.

Don't Worry About Chapter/Verse Breakdowns Until After You Know the Words

First of all, you need to decide if knowing the chapter and verse references is important to you. I have decided that knowing the *chapter* where I can find a verse is important, but knowing all the specific verse references is less important. If someone wants to know where to find the story of "Jesus Feeding 5000 People" or "The Death and Resurrection of Lazarus," I want to be able to point them to John 6 and John 11. I find it less crucial to say, "John 6:1-15 and John 11:1-44."

I do know several people however who find it extremely important to know the verses as well as the chapters. You simply need to decide how specific you want to get. Whichever you choose, the most important thing is to internalize in the correct order:

Overall message...
Then individual stories/thoughts...
Then paragraphs...
Then verses.

If you follow this pattern – which is built into this entire Bible study process – you will find that knowing the chapters simply comes with moving through Foundation, Framing and Finish Work. Learning the verse references will need to be an extra step you add on if you deem that to be important.

Don't Try to Internalize Something You Do Not Know

Now, this might seem obvious if you are weaving Scripture Internalization into your study of an entire book. However, there may be times when you want to learn an individual verse or paragraph that has special meaning for you. My encouragement at times like these is to make sure you spend some time familiarizing yourself with the surrounding context.

Let's say you want to learn II Peter 1:3-4:

> "His divine power has given us everything we need for life and godliness through our knowledge of him who called us by his own glory and goodness. Through these he has given us his very great and precious promises, so that through them you may participate in the divine nature and escape the corruption in the world caused by evil desires."

Before learning these verses, it will be extremely helpful for you to take even a few days and apply Foundational Reading techniques to II Peter. As you become a bit more familiar with the letter, you will find that even these two verses hold greater meaning for you because you know the context in which they were written. Who knows? You might even find yourself making II Peter the next book you choose to study and internalize!

IS IT REALLY POSSIBLE TO GET THE WORDS IN THE RIGHT ORDER?

General and Specific Techniques

☨

I n the introduction to this book, I mentioned a man named Bruce Kuhn who was the first person I ever saw "perform" a book of the Bible. As we talked over lunch the day after we met, Bruce said something I will never forget. I had just asked him the same question I now get asked more than any other question: How do you memorize that many verses? He simply said, "Memorize the story first. Then, use the words on the page to tell the story."

"Memorizing the story" takes place naturally as you move from Foundation through Framing and Finish Work. As you apply the principles described in this book, you will find that you thoroughly know the "story" of the book you are studying. It will become like an old friend. Not only will you not forget it, but you will find yourself returning to it again and again for fresh insight.

At this point, you will have what I call a "working knowledge" of the book, and some of you may choose to stop here. You know where to find certain verses. You know the author's thought process. You know the overall themes as well as the individual ideas. You probably know several portions word-for-word, but you do not know the whole book yet.

This chapter provides you with some general and specific techniques for taking the next step of internalization and getting the words in the right order. Whether you apply these to a single story, a chapter, or an entire book of the Bible is up to you. I have found that the general techniques are effective for almost everybody, no matter the style or length of the passage being internalized. As I have taught *Falling in Love with God's Word* over the years, I have also compiled some specific techniques that have proven helpful to many people. While I have tried them all, I have found the ones that work best for me and stuck with those. As you try the different techniques, you will likely find yourself drawn to a few as well. The Bible may be "one size fits all," but the techniques for learning the words will vary depending on your preferences and learning style.

As I mentioned in the introduction to this section, this part of the internalization process does not fit into the timeframe of a 60-Day Adventure. For some, applying these principles for a couple of weeks will be enough to learn the entire book. For others, a month or two is more realistic. It all depends on how perfectly you desire to know it, how much internalization you have done in the past, and how much time and effort you have to invest in the process. Whatever your specific situation, you will surely find that any amount of time spent internalizing God's Word will bring forth exponential benefit in your everyday life. Once we have done the work of "planting" the words of Scripture in our minds, the Holy Spirit can then access His Word to encourage, challenge, teach, and comfort us.

General Technique 1: Use the same Bible.

I mentioned this briefly in the chapter on Foundational Reading. If you are trying to keep the words straight, it is important

143

to use not only the same translation, but the same physical Bible. Choose a translation, grab a Bible, and stick to it!

As you read the same Bible, you will begin to remember where different phrases, stories, and verses appear on the page. You will actually begin to visualize verses as part of the overall story, rather than merely as a list of words to be arranged in the right order. You will remember where a story physically begins and where it ends. For example, as I write this I can picture the story of the healing of the blind man (John 9) beginning halfway down the first column on the right-hand page in my Bible. The same thing will happen for you. The consistent locations of these verses and paragraphs will continually reinforce them in your mind.

General Technique 2: Read with your eyes closed.

This may sound strange, but bear with me. Once you find that you are quite familiar with a passage, try closing your eyes after reading the first several words in the sentence. This will be much easier if you start by reading out loud. Picture the page in your mind's eye and continue to "read" the passage. Continue reading with your eyes closed, following the verses on the "page" in your mind until you simply cannot go any further. Open your eyes only long enough to get yourself back on track. Again close your eyes and keep reading.

You will be surprised at how far you can go without looking at the page. In fact, whenever you *do* need to open your eyes, you will find that your eyes will go to the exact point on the page where you got stuck. Why? Because they have seen those words – in that place

– so many times before. The more frequently you do this, the further you will be able to read with your eyes closed.

General Technique 3: Read with your Bible closed.

Once you have reached the point where you spend a lot more time with your eyes closed than open, try "reading" the passage before you even open your Bible. If you get stuck, pause for a few seconds and try to mentally get yourself back on track without opening your Bible. Think about where you are in the story. See if focusing on the *elements* of the story reminds you of the words. Then go back a couple of sentences and take another run at it.

If you find you simply cannot get going again, open your Bible, get yourself started again and close your Bible. Notice that I did not say, "Use your finger as a bookmark for the next time you get stuck." Don't do it! If you do, you will cheat too quickly the next time. You need to allow yourself to think through the spots that are difficult for you. You do not want to train your mind to get stuck every time you hit a certain phrase or passage.

As you integrate these general techniques into your Bible study, every piece of the study process will reinforce the words for you. Reading and rereading. Learning about the characters and background. Writing general and specific outlines. Word studies. Life application. The more you get to know the story, the more you will be able to "tell the story using the words on the page."

Specific Technique 1: Listen to audio tapes or CDs

Many people find it helpful to have audio tapes of the Scripture passages they want to internalize. These can be used at any stage in the internalization process. Early on, audio tapes can be another way to picture the story as you drive your car, wash the dishes, take a shower, or mow the lawn. As you get to know the passage better, you can speak along with an audio tape and notice where you leave out a word or say the wrong word entirely.

Any Christian bookstore will have audio recordings of the Bible. You can purchase a set of tapes or CDs with the entire Bible read in almost any of the major translations. Before buying an audio Bible, make sure it is the same translation as your study Bible. If possible, see if the store has a sample for you to listen to. Some audio Bibles are read by one speaker; others have multiple actors reading the various parts. Each audio Bible will also have varying amounts of dramatic style incorporated (background music, sound effects, etc.). You need to make sure you are buying a Bible that you will actually enjoy listening to!

If you do not want to buy an entire audio Bible, you can also make your own. When our small group was studying Galatians, I simply grabbed a blank tape and recorded myself reading Galatians. This is an inexpensive alternative that will keep things very simple.

Specific Technique 2: Use note cards and sticky notes.

People have used this technique for years to remember just about anything and it can certainly be helpful for learning the

Bible as well – particularly the parts that get us tongue-tied. For every book I have learned, I have found there are always a handful of verses I either leave out or have a hard time keeping straight. If you find the same is true for you, write that verse (or verses) on a sticky note and put it in a place where you will see it several times a day. This may be a bathroom mirror, closet door, refrigerator, or the dashboard of your car. You can also write it on a note card and keep it in your brief case or day timer, or on your desk at work. There have even been times where I have used a Bible verse as a "scrolling screensaver" on my computer screen. Be creative! Just put it where you will see it.

Specific Technique 3: Learning lists.

All throughout the Bible, we find lists. Lists of names, characteristics, and cities, just to name a few. Learning these lists and keeping the words in the right order can seem overwhelming. For an example of how to make this manageable, let's take a look at the list in Philippians 4:8.

> *Finally, brothers, whatever is **true**, whatever is **noble**, whatever is **right**, whatever is **pure**, whatever is **lovely**, whatever is **admirable** – if anything is **excellent** or **praiseworthy** – think about such things.* **(emphasis mine)**

I have highlighted here the eight items that make up this list. First, check to see if there is any obvious pattern. Throughout the

Bible there are lists where words right next to each other start with the same letter. Other times it just so happens that the words are in alphabetical order. I have even noticed that some lists have words that rhyme. If any of these are true for the list you are trying to learn, make a mental note of the pattern. Our brains love patterns. We learn patterns quickly, and can remember them for a long time.

The list in the verse above has no obvious pattern. When this is the case, there are several other techniques that have helped me greatly. The first is to group items together. Notice that the first six items in the list all start with "whatever is..." Rather than trying to remember six individual items, simply turn those first six words into two groups of three items. "True-noble-right" becomes one item and "pure-lovely-admirable" is the second. "Excellent-praiseworthy" is a third item of its own. Once these groupings begin to flow off your tongue, you have reduced the number of items to remember from eight to three!

The second technique is to reduce the list even further by simply remembering the first letter of each word. Now the groupings are "t-n-r," "p-l-a," and "e-p." At this point, you have read the verse enough times that you know the words. You simply need a mental trigger that will tell your mind what order to put the words in.

There is one other technique that could help you with lists. If you ever took piano lessons as a kid, you will catch on to this one right away. When I first started to take lessons, my piano teacher wanted me to learn the notes on the sheet music. She told me that each line represented a note. If she would have said, "The first line is E, the second is G, then B, then D, and finally F" I probably would have forgotten them as quickly as she said them. Instead, she had me say along with her, "Every Good Boy Deserves Fudge." As an eight-year-old boy, that stuck with me!

You can do the same thing with word lists found in the Bible. For example, you could take Philippians 4:8 and say, "The New Royal Prince Loves An Extraordinary Princess." If you read Philippians 4:8 ten times and then repeat the above sentence five more times, you will most likely never forget this verse! Anything you can do to create a pattern or word association will help you remember lists easier than ever before.

Specific Technique 4: Write it out.

I have a friend who has internalized more Scripture than anyone else I know. One of his favorite things to do after he knows a passage pretty well is to simply write it out. He takes out a pencil and paper and just starts writing. He even tries to keep the line and page breaks in the same places as in his Bible so that he is reinforcing what his eye has seen while reading. He also finds that this is a tremendous opportunity to meditate on Scripture. Since we write slower than we read, we can "soak in" every word we write, rather than simply skimming through.

Try this a time or two. You might find that typing the words into your computer works better for you. Or you might want to include sections of Scripture in your journal. Whatever you choose, you might just find – as my friend did – that writing out the words of Scripture not only helped him remember it better, but drew him into a more intimate relationship with the Author.

Specific Technique 5: Use a Scripture memory program for
your computer.

Not too long ago I typed the phrase "Scripture memorization"
into an Internet search engine. I was amazed at the amount of
information I found. There were links to websites about Scripture
memory organizations, groups, clubs, and camps. Individuals created sites telling about the impact of Scripture internalization on
their lives and how they go about doing it.

Along the way, I found several websites devoted to software
that helps people internalize Scripture. Some of these software programs can be ordered, while others are available for free. I down-
loaded a few of them and tried them out. Some were pretty good
and others were not as helpful.

I would like to warn you that the programs I found were focused
on learning one section or verse at a time. None were designed to
help someone internalize a large passage – let alone an entire book.
Having said that, I think these programs could still be very useful
for helping you learn a passage that is particularly meaningful to
you or that you are having difficulty with.

Most of these programs guide you through learning and reviewing the verses already in the program. Only a few will actually allow
you to enter in your own verses.

Since software is continuously created and updated, I am not
going to recommend a certain program here. If you think one of
these programs might be a helpful tool to add to your repertoire of
Scripture internalization tools, I encourage you to go online and
search around. It took me less than an hour to find more informa-

tion than I could sift through in a month. Most of the programs that were for sale had trials you could download and experiment with before placing an order.

Specific Technique 6: Have someone else check you.

This is an extremely effective technique, but it rarely gets used. Why? Because having someone else check you can be nerve-wracking. I highly encourage you to give it a try though. Maybe you could even find a partner who would be your "internalization buddy" and learn the same passages you are learning at the same time.

There are two different ways to have someone check you. The first is to have them simply keep track of your mistakes without stopping you. Let them write down the verses you stumble over. They can also note times when you slow down or become so focused on the words that the message is unclear. This will immediately show you which verses need a little extra work and review.

The second method is to have your listener stop you every time you make a mistake or stumble over a verse. Since it is counterproductive to stop every two verses, make sure you save this method until after you know the passage quite well. This falls into the category of "fine tuning." When your partner stops you and has you redo a verse, you will avoid practicing a verse incorrectly.

I should let you know that practicing with a partner can be both extremely rewarding and extremely frustrating. When your partner stops you at the exact same verse for making the same mistake for the tenth time in a row, you may very well want to throw something at them. (Let me suggest a pillow, as opposed to your

Bible or a lamp.) However, as you both find yourselves falling in love with the same portion of God's Word, you will enjoy Scripture more than ever!

✝

There are many other specific "tips and tricks" for learning Scripture. If you know someone who has internalized quite a bit, ask them how they do it. Take a trip to your local bookstore – or search online – and see what else you can find. The first thing you'll want to do is start employing the general techniques right away. Then experiment with several specific techniques and find the ones that produce the best results for you. The key is to find what works and then stick to it.

Now that It is in My Brain... How Do I Keep It There?

Review

†

After putting in the effort to thoroughly internalize a portion of Scripture, you probably want to be sure that it stays with you. I have yet, however, to discover a way to learn something once and have it forever cemented in my memory. (If you happen to figure this one out, please let the rest of us in on it.)

In fact, almost anything we ever learn – not just the Bible – requires some review if we are going to be able to access the information in the future. For example, how well can you still speak the foreign language you studied for two, three, or even four years in high school and college? After taking French for three years in high school and one year in college, I actually *lived* in France for one semester in college. I never became fluent, but by the end of that trip, I could easily get around Paris, shop, order at a restaurant, and have everyday conversations with my host family. Now, more than fifteen years later, I would be lucky to leave a French restaurant without offending the waiter, let alone having ordered something edible.

Bottom line: *You must review anything you want to remember.* Period. This chapter is dedicated to helping you find a method of review that works for you, as well as maximizes the time you spend. The four recommendations that follow will help you do just that.

First – Review Often

This is a very simple concept that applies to anything you are learning, whether it is a Scripture passage, a musical instrument, or a foreign language. If you spend ten minutes a day in review, Monday through Friday, you will remember far more than if you limit your review time to two hours every Saturday. We all have little windows of time built into our days. Twenty minutes driving to work. Three minutes walking out to get the mail. Seven minutes in the shower. Two minutes brushing your teeth. (Let me suggest silent review at this point. It could get messy.)

I am not suggesting you fill every spare minute with Bible review. There are certainly times when we need to notice things around us, spend extra moments in prayer, or simply take a mental break. If we pay attention to our daily routines, however, we will notice opportunities when reviewing Scripture can help us refocus on the God who wrote His Word especially to draw us closer to Him.

Second – Review FAST for FLUIDITY

Fast review can be particularly effective for those small "windows" just discussed in the previous paragraphs. When there is not much time to truly meditate on Scripture, fast review can make sure the words stay in our brains and flow off our tongues.

This kind of review is done exactly as it sounds – fast. This is not the time to focus on the meaning, emotion, punctuation, and application. This is only review of the words.

Begin saying the passage as quickly as you can without jumbling the words. As you move through the passage, make a mental note of places you stumble or slow down. Later, work on those sections until you can move through them with the same fluidity you have in the rest of the passage.

Fast review can significantly enhance the next two review methods: Medium and Slow. As the words flow easily off your tongue, you will have a greater ability to remember the message and meditate on the specifics without constantly thinking about which words come next.

Third – Review at MEDIUM Speed to Remember the MESSAGE

When you review at medium speed, pretend you are telling someone a story. This is the exact same speed I use whenever I am presenting a book of the Bible. The focus at this point is the *message*. You want to hear and tell this story (or letter) just as the original author might if he was in the room.

In order to do this, you can ask yourself a few questions as you begin to review at medium speed. For example, if you are reviewing Philippians, you might ask: what would it have felt like for Paul to sit in prison and write this letter? Was he happy, frustrated, or angry with the Philippians? How did his emotions change as he moved from point to point? What did he want his readers to come away with after reading this letter?

Be sure to keep all the emotion in the passage as you review. Sometimes this is easy. Other times it can present a challenge. There will even be times when you are not quite sure what emotion to use. My suggestion? Try it several different ways and see what feels right. If you are comfortable, get someone else's feedback as you share the passage with them.

The more you review at medium speed, the more *real* the passage will become to you. Different things will jump out at different times. You will be *experiencing* Scripture, rather than just reading it. By the way, you will be experiencing it in much the same way the early church did!

Fourth – Review SLOWLY to Meditate on the SPECIFICS

Over and over I have discovered that it is in times of slow review that God seems to speak to me most. As you weave slow review into your Bible study, you will likely find specific details, words, emotions, and phrases that you never noticed before.

At this point, you have moved beyond focusing on the order of the words. Your time spent in study, fast review, and medium review has made the words flow. You can now shift to meditating on God's Word. Force yourself to meander slowly through a passage. If you are doing this in one of those "windows" of time we mentioned earlier, you might only get through a verse or two. Terrific! The goal here is not covering territory, but connecting with your Creator.

At this time, allow yourself to dig a little deeper into the questions you asked during medium review. Picture every character in the story. Who is he? What does she look like? What expression is on his face? How did she feel as this was taking place? Place yourself in the scene. What are the sights, sounds, smells, tastes, and physical sensations? Go beyond seeing with your mind's eye to tasting with your mind's mouth and smelling with your mind's nose. Let these stories become a part of you.

If you are studying a letter – like Philippians – read each phrase as if it was written in a letter specifically to you. What would it be like to have someone write these words to you? What words and phrases jump out at you? There will be different words that speak to you on different days and at different times in your life.

Slow review can be a simple two-minute connecting point between you and God in the midst of a busy day. Or, it can be woven into a longer time of study and prayer. I encourage you to do both. Allow God to speak to you through His Word. Allow Him to reveal Himself to you. Allow Him to challenge, teach, encourage, and comfort you. Even after you have spent days, weeks, or months immersed in a book, slow review will reveal things to you that you never noticed before. After all, that is why we call it the Living Word of God.

✝

As with internalization, review doesn't fit into a specific time-line of ten, thirty, or sixty days. Our brains are all wired differently. We all need review, but some of us need more than others. If your desire is to remember a fairly lengthy passage word-for-word, you might need to review it once a week. Someone else might be able to review every month or so and still be able to keep it all straight. As you go through the process of learning the passage, you will get a very good feel for how much review you need. For me, I know there are certain books I need to review often, while others seem to stick with me with much less effort.

The key is to utilize all three methods of review – fast, medium, and slow – and see which ones help the most and how frequently you need to make use of each method. However frequently you end up reviewing Scripture, you will surely find it drawing you closer to God's heart.

FINAL
THOUGHTS

I nevitably there will be some who read *Falling in Love with God's Word* who have already been studying the Bible for years, while others will be using it as a starting point. Wherever you are on your "Bible study journey," I pray you have found some practical help that can be applied right away.

Developing a love for God and His Word is the most exciting, beneficial endeavor you could ever undertake. Whether you jump right into the 60-day Adventure in Philippians, apply the principals of Foundational Reading, or simply add a few Word Studies to your current study habits, my desire is that your enjoyment of the Bible and devotion to the Author will increase because you have spent time in these pages. I also hope that you will return to *Falling in Love with God's Word* as a reference as you study. I know how much these techniques have revolutionized my love for the Bible. I pray the same happens for you.

Developing a lasting, enriching relationship with God and His Word is a lifelong journey. A journey of developing King David's attitude toward God's Word. *"Oh, how I love your Law! I meditate on it all day long."* (Psalm 119:97) A journey of moving the words on the page to our life in the world. A journey of allowing God's Word to transform our minds and saturate our hearts. A journey of becoming "Word-filled" believers. A journey God can't wait for you to take. A journey that will be challenging at times, but will always be worth the effort. A journey I am on with you. A journey of falling in love with God's Word!

Embrace the journey!
Keith

APPENDIXES

A. *Applying It All: A 60-day Adventure in Philippians*
B. *Suggestions for New Believers*
C. *A Guide for Small Groups*

APPLYING IT ALL: A 60-DAY ADVENTURE IN PHILIPPIANS[1]

Appendix A

Foundation & Framing

1. Read Philippians
2. Read Philippians
3. Read Philippians
4. Read Philippians as if you were Paul
5. Read Philippians – BS on the Author
6. Read Philippians in a different version
7. Read Philippians
8. Read Philippians as if you were a member of the Philippian church
9. Read Philippians – BS on the Audience
10. Read Philippians – Write a rough draft PU
11. Read Philippians – Write a rough draft FO
12. Read Philippians
13. Read Philippians – BS on the Atmosphere
14. Read Philippians in a different version
15. Read Philippians – Review PU
16. Read Philippians – Review FO
17. Read Philippians – BS on the Purpose
18. Read Philippians
19. Read Philippians
20. Read Philippians – Review PU
21. Read Philippians – Review FO
22. Read Philippians in a different version
23. Read Philippians
24. Read Philippians
25. Read Philippians – Final Draft of PU
26. Read Philippians – Final Draft of FO
27. Read Philippians Chapter One carefully – Write an FR of Chapter One
28. Read Philippians Chapter Two carefully – Write an FRof Chapter Two
29. Read Philippians Chapter Three carefully – Write an FR of Chapter Three
30. Read Philippians Chapter Four carefully – Write an FR of Chapter Four

BS = Background Study	PM = Paragraph Map
PU = Purpose Statement	PS = Paragraph Summary
FO = Foundation Outline	WS = Word/Phrase Study
FR = Framing Outline	LA = Life Application

Finish Work
31. PM – 1:1-2; WS – "servant"
32. PM – 1:3-6; WS – "joy," LA – 1:3-6
33. PM – 1:7-8; LA 1:7-8
34. PM – 1:9-11; WS "pure" LA – 1:9-11
35. PS – 1:12-14
36. PM – 1:15-18a; WS – "selfish ambition"
37. LA – 1:15-18a
38. PM – 1:18b-26
39. WS – "hope"; LA 1:18b-26
40. Read Philippians
41. PM – 1:27-30; WS – "stand"; LA 1:27-30
42. PM – 2:1-4; WS – "fellowship"
43. LA – 2:1-4; WS – "humility"
44. PM – 2:5-11; WS – "nature" (compare verse 6 with verse 7 – different Greek words)
45. LA – 2:5-11
46. PM – 2:12-13 & 14-18; WS – "work out"
47. LA – 2:12-13 & 14-18; WS – "drink offering"
48. PS – 2:19-24; LA – 2:19-24
49. PS – 2:25-30; WS – "honor"; LA – 2:25-30
50. Read Philippians
51. PM – 3:1, 2-4a, & 4b-6; WS – "safeguard"; LA – 3:1-6
52. PM – 3:7-11; WS – "rubbish"
53. LA   3:7-11; WS – "righteousness"
54. PM – 3:12-14 & 15-16; WS – "press on"; LA – 3:12-16
55. PM – 3:17-4:1; WS – "citizenship"; LA – 3:17-4:1
56. PS – 4:2-3; PM – 4:4-7 & 8-9; WS – "anxious"
57. LA – 4:2-9; WS any word from list in Verse 8
58. PM – 4:10-13 & 14-20; WS – "content"
59. LA – 4:10-20; WS – "amply supplied"
60. PM – 4:21-23; LA – 4:21-23; Read Philippians

SUGGESTIONS FOR NEW BELIEVERS

Appendix B

First of all, let me say, "Welcome to the family!" Following Jesus and serving God will not be easy, but it will be the most wonderful journey you could ever take. If we are going to live lives that are pleasing to God, we need to know what He has done *for* us, what He expects *from* us, and what He wants to do *through* us. God gave us the Bible specifically to reveal these things to us, and I pray this book will help you to fall in love with God's Word.

This book simply outlines one of the many methods for studying the Bible. Before you dive right into the 60-Day Adventure in Philippians (Appendix A), allow me to make three recommendations that will provide a good launching pad for you when it comes to studying – and loving – the Bible.

One: Find a good church.

Talk to friends and family about a good church in your area. Believers need to be connected so they can worship together, encourage one another, and help each other grow.

It is essential to find a church with people you can relate to, musical worship that draws you closer to God, and a pastor who teaches the Bible with enthusiasm. If at all possible, find a church that has a small group ministry so that you can connect on a deeper level with a handful of people. It can often be too easy for a new believer to get "lost in the crowd." You need to find a place where you can plant yourself and grow.

Two: Find a Bible study partner.

If you have a friend – or small group – who will study the same part of the Bible you are studying, you will find it easier to be consistent and you will enjoy having someone to discuss new insights and questions with. A church small group is perfect for this. If you are unable to get into a small group right now, see if you can at least find one other person who will encourage you in your study and make sure you are sticking to it. Remember: You are trying to build a new habit into your life that has never been there before. Just like eating right or exercising, it is much easier to quit if you are on your own – and much more enjoyable if you have a partner.

Three: A suggestion for where to start reading.

As I am sure you have noticed, the Bible is a pretty long book. I have heard many different suggestions as to the best place for a young believer to start. Some would say, "Start at the beginning – Genesis." Others would offer their favorite book in the New Testament. For a new believer, however, I feel the best way to start this journey is to get to know Jesus as well as possible and learn about the ways other people lived as they came to know Him.

Fortunately, God has given us four different books of the Bible that are specifically about the life of Jesus (Matthew, Mark, Luke, and John) and another book about the life of the believers in the early years of Christianity (Acts). These are the first five books of the New Testament. Everything in the Old Testament happened before Jesus came to earth. Everything in the New Testament happened while He was here and after He lived on earth.

Matthew, Mark, Luke, and John are called the gospels (a word that simply means "Good News"). They are biographies of Christ from the perspectives of four different people. Just as you can read several biographies about a former president or athlete and find different information, the same is true here. While these books do not contradict each other, there are some parts of Jesus' life that appear in only one gospel, some that appear in two or three, and some that appear in all four.

Acts (also known as Acts of the Apostles) was written by Luke, the same man who wrote the third gospel. He recorded the lives of Peter (one of Jesus' original disciples), Paul (author of most books in the New Testament), and many other early believers. Acts gives a good picture of the early church and the ways that first century Christians spread the good news about Jesus.

Now, here is my suggestion. Start by deciding how much time each day you will spend reading. Thirty minutes? Twenty minutes? Ten? Choose a time and commit to it.

Now start with one of the gospels and simply read it as you would a novel. (NOTE: I have listed the gospels in the order they appear in the Bible, not in order of importance. Any of them is a wonderful starting place. Feel free to pick one, or ask a friend or pastor for a suggestion.) As you read, get to know the characters, storyline, and recurring themes, as well as the ways Jesus interacted with people and the ways people reacted to Jesus. Look at Jesus' statements about Himself and the way we should live. Picture yourself in the story.

When you finish this gospel, skip over and read Acts next. Read it the same way you read the first book – as a novel. After reading Acts, read another gospel. After that read Acts again. Then the third gospel. Then Acts. Then the fourth gospel. Then Acts once more.

By the time you finish, you will have read about the life of Jesus from four different perspectives and you will have also read about the life of the early church four times. As you can see from the chart below, if you commit to reading five days a week for twenty minutes each day, it will take about three months to do this. If you only feel like you can commit to ten minutes a day for four days each week, you will still finish in less than seven months. That may seem like a long time, but those seven months will give you a foundation of knowledge that will be priceless when it comes to understanding and enjoying the Bible for the rest of your life.

Reading Chart

Total Reading Time	10 min. per day	20 min. per day
Matthew – 2h 40m	16 days	8 days
Mark – 1h 20m	8 days	4 days
Luke – 3h	18 days	8 days
John – 2h	12 days	6 days
Acts – 2h 40m	16 days	8 days

After reading the Gospels and Acts in this fashion you will be ready to try the 60-Day Adventure (see Appendix A). If you choose to study a book other than Philippians you can still apply the principles outlined in this book. By that time, you might have received some recommendations from a friend or pastor, or you may even be involved in a small group that is studying the Bible together. In any event, you will be well on your way to falling in love with God's Word.

A Guide for
Small Groups

Appendix C

†

The principles of the Foundation, Framing, Finish Work study method can be adapted very successfully for use in small groups. Naturally, a group setting brings a new dynamic to the study. In any study group, you will find some people who are committed to studying the Bible everyday, while others will spend a few days a week in the Word. Still others will be brand new to Bible study, and will be just developing the habit of personal Bible study.

For most groups, the 60-Day Adventure in Philippians found in Appendix A would be overwhelming to some members of the group. You may, however, be part of a small group that desires that high level of commitment. Just make sure that you are all on the same page before beginning your study.

Following is an outline for studying Ephesians we used in our small group. Of course, the concept can be applied to any book your group chooses to study. Our group chose to have a different couple "lead" the discussion each week, but it would work equally well to establish a leader who would facilitate throughout the duration of the study.

Week One

The first week, we all committed to reading Ephesians at least four times. Some members of the group decided to read everyday, but the commitment was to at least four complete readings of Ephesians.

We established that our first week's discussion would focus on the general ideas in Ephesians – *not* on the specific verses. During this week, we incorporated principles of Foundational Reading and Background Studies, and we answered questions such as: What can we learn about the relationship between Paul and the church in Ephesus from this letter? Was Paul happy with them? Frustrated? Sad? Is this an encouraging letter? What would it have felt like to receive this letter? Those group members who were interested also had the option of looking into Bible dictionaries, the Internet and any other resources to learn about the author, audience and atmosphere of Ephesians. For further ideas, see the chapters on Foundational Reading and Background Studies.

Week Two and Three

During both of these weeks, we continued the process of reading the entire letter to the Ephesians at least four times each week, but we changed the focus of our discussions. During week two we narrowed our discussion to the first three chapters of Ephesians. Week three was devoted to chapters four through six. Any notes we took during our personal time were to be limited to the half of the book we would be discussing the following week.

Our discussions ranged from overall concepts and messages to sections that seemed unclear. Some members would share portions that were especially meaningful to them or applicable to something they were going through at that time.

Weeks Four through Nine

Each of the following six weeks was dedicated to a single chapter. We still set a goal of reading Ephesians in its entirety at least once during the week, but most days were to be spent meditating on the message of a single chapter.

When we all came together, we each shared certain verses that had special meaning to us, as well as the specific life applications God placed on our hearts. These focused discussions also allowed us to address questions we had encountered in our personal study time. In addition, the designated leaders for the week prepared a few appropriate questions in order to keep everyone moving in the same direction.

Week Ten

To conclude our study in Ephesians, our group spent one final week discussing Ephesians as a whole. We again committed to reading Ephesians at least four times in its entirety, and we then talked about new insights we had gained and any questions we still had. Taking a week to simply read Ephesians again (after six weeks of digging deep) was a terrific way to end the study. We really saw how much our understanding of Ephesians had grown since those first couple of weeks. We were also able to summarize the lessons we had learned and the applications we had made – and were continuing to make.

SMALL GROUP OVERVIEW

Week One

- Read Ephesians at least four times
- Keep discussion limited to the book as a whole (purpose, background, etc.)

Week Two

- Read Ephesians at least four times
- Limit discussion to Ephesians 1-3

Week Three

- Read Ephesians at least four times
- Limit discussion to Ephesians 4-6

Weeks Four through Nine

- Read Ephesians at least once, each week, in its entirety
- Read the chapter of focus everyday
- Focus discussion on one chapter only
- Discuss meaningful verses, life applications, and questions

Week Ten

- Read Ephesians at least four times
- Recap what you learned in Weeks One through Nine
- Address any final thoughts or questions

This outline can – and should – be modified to fit the style of your group or the length of time your group wants to study a single book. I have heard of one group that dedicated an entire year to the book of Ephesians. They spent the first several weeks "setting the stage." They applied the concepts of Foundational Reading and looked at the overall purpose of Ephesians. They did Background Studies, looking at all the information they could find about Ephesus, Paul, and the culture at the time. However, by the end of the year, they were looking at only a few verses each week.

No matter how in-depth your group decides to go, you will find studying a book as a group will prove very worthwhile and enjoyable. You will gain tremendous insight from group discussions. Since you will be sharing applications, you will know how to purposely pray for each other. Knowing that others are studying with you will be an encouragement to be more consistent. You will also find that your whole group is *falling in love with God's Word* at the same time.

NOTES

Introduction

1. Robert Shirock has since edited and retitled *Mastering the Bible Book by Book*. It is currently published as *Transformed by the Renewing of Your Mind: A Radical Daily Method of Bible Study* (Plymouth: Jubilee Publishing, 2003). I am grateful to Bob for   writing down this method in a way that has had a profound, lifelong impact on developing my love for God's Word.

Setting the Stage

1. Robert Shirock, *Transformed by the Renewing of Your Mind: A Radical Daily Method of Bible Study* (Plymouth: Jubilee Publishing, 2003), p13-17.

Foundation

1. The concepts found in these chapters on Foundation (Foundational Reading, Background Studies, and Purpose Statement) were first put forth by James Gray and described as "synthetic" study – a way of putting everything together before analyzing it in detail. He wrote of this approach in *How to Master the English Bible: an Experience, a Method, a Result, an Illustration*, first published in 1904. It was later republished by Moody Press in 1951. In 2000, it was edited and updated by Shawn Boutwell and printed by Binford & Mort, Portland, Oregon. This approach of synthetic study was also written about by G. Campbell Morgan in *The Study and Teaching of the English Bible*, (London: James Clark & Co., 1910). I first read about the Synthetic Method in Robert Shirock's book, *Transformed by the Renewing of Your Mind: A Radical Daily Method of Bible Study* (Plymouth: Jubilee Publishing, 2003).

Foundational Reading

1. Concepts 1-4: James Gray, *How to Master the English Bible: an Experience, a Method, a Result, an Illustration* (Chicago: The Bible Institute Coportage Association, 1904), p.44-55. Concept 5: Robert Shirock, *Transformed by the Renewing of Your Mind: A Radical Daily Method of Bible Study* (Plymouth: Jubilee Publishing, 2003), p.38-39.

Foundation Outline

1. The Foundation Outline is an adaptation of the "Synthetic Outline" discussed by Robert Shirock, *Transformed by the Renewing of Your Mind: A Radical Daily Method of Bible Study* (Plymouth: Jubilee Publishing, 2003), p.42-43.

Framing Outline

1. The Framing Outline is an adaptation of the "Analytical Outline" discussed by Robert Shirock, *Transformed by the Renewing of Your Mind: A Radical Daily Method of Bible Study* (Plymouth: Jubilee Publishing, 2003), p.55-58.

Paragraphs

1. This approach to studying paragraphs (and words and phrases in the next chapter) is adapted from Robert Shirock, *Transformed by the Renewing of Your Mind: A Radical Daily Method of Bible Study* (Plymouth: Jubilee Publishing, 2003), Chapters 5 and 6.

2. Shirock, p. 64

Life Application

1. The American Heritage® Dictionary of the English Language, Third Edition copyright © 1992 by Houghton Mifflin Company. Electronic version licensed from INSO Corporation; further reproduction and distribution restricted in accordance with the Copyright Law of the United States. All rights reserved.

2. The American Heritage® Dictionary of the English Language.

Five Reasons

1. Chuck Swindoll, *Seasons of Life*, (Grand Rapids: Zondervan, 1994), p.54

Appendix A

1. When I was first shown this method I was challenged to do the "60-Day Experiment in II Timothy" in the back of *Mastering the Bible Book by Book*, by Robert Shirock. This appendix is an adaptation of that method applied to Philippians and utilizing the new format and terminology.

ABOUT THE AUTHOR

Keith Ferrin founded That You May Know Ministries in 1996 and has since traveled throughout the United States and internationally as a conference speaker, storyteller, dramatist, and worship leader. He spent six years as a youth and worship pastor prior to traveling full-time.

Keith received a Bachelor of Arts degree in Psychology from Pacific Lutheran University and went on to earn a Master of Education in Guidance and Counseling.

When he's not on the road, Keith enjoys hiking, soccer, movies, and going to Mariner's baseball games. Most of all, Keith likes spending time at the waterfront with his wife, Kari, and their newest addition, Sarah Elizabeth.

Keith, Kari, and Sarah live in Kirkland, Washington, just outside of Seattle.